new
upholstery

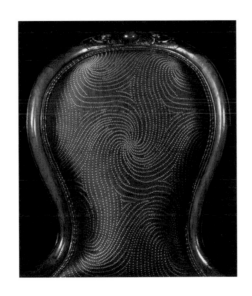

new upholstery

nicole fulton
with stuart weston

MITCHELL BEAZLEY

First published in Great Britain in 2004
by Mitchell Beazley, an imprint of Octopus
Publishing Group Ltd, 2–4 Heron Quays,
London E14 4JP

Reprinted 2006

ISBN-13: 978-1-84000-856-2
ISBN-10: 1-84000-856-3

A CIP record of this book is available from
the British Library

Senior Executive Editor **Anna Sanderson**
Executive Art Editor **Auberon Hedgecoe**
Art Director **Vivienne Brar**
Designer **Colin Goody**
Photographer **Roger Dixon**
Illustrator **Carolyn Jenkins**
Project Editors **Karen Hemingway**
                Catherine Emslie
Copy Editor **Jo Weeks**
Picture Researcher **Jenny Faithfull**
Proofreader **Lara Maiklem**
Indexer **Hilary Bird**
Production controller **Gary Hayes**

Set in Gill Sans

Colour reproduction by Fine Arts, Hong Kong
Printed and bound in China by Toppan

contents

introduction

This book explores individual styles and shapes of furniture, focusing on reupholstering them in innovative and non-traditional ways. Taking vintage, period, and more modern pieces of furniture, *New Upholstery* aims to transform each piece, giving it a new lease of life. Rather than consider more traditional fabrics such as chintzes, florals, and tapestries, *New Upholstery* indulges in the great choice of fabulous contemporary fabrics now available. A late nineteenth-century button-back chair is reupholstered in a warm, taupe wool, a balloon-back chair is reupholstered in sensuous pony skin, and an original Arts and Crafts chair is reupholstered in bold cream and chocolate brown geometric patterned silk. New pieces of furniture are also introduced, simple round footstools upholstered in two different treatments, headboards and screens are made from scratch and covered in sumptuous, vibrant fabrics, and vintage pieces such as an original G Plan chair are stripped of their old velour and recovered in soft, pebble-coloured leather.

There are now a great many fabric styles to choose from and be inspired by. *New Upholstery* looks at a selection of the more contemporary fabrics, considering colour, texture, and patterns and suggests different ways of combining these. The overall shape and style of a piece of furniture is also discussed, looking at how best to bring out the character in a piece using different fabrics. Trimmings and finishes are considered, showing how a simple trimming can change the whole look of a piece. Choosing the right fabric, whether it is sumptuous velvet, plain linen, wool, or cowhide, can transform a piece, giving it a very different look.

Sourcing interesting and beautiful furniture is also covered, concentrating on what to look for in a piece, including the shape of leg, the quality of the show wood, and its overall character.

Upholstery is both a practical skill and an art form that has developed over the centuries. It continues to evolve as new working materials and new techniques are introduced. This book provides substantial practical information on the traditional methods but also focuses on some more modern techniques where appropriate. Typically a period piece of furniture is best upholstered using traditional methods such as hand-stitched stuffing and using a hammer and tacks, thereby maintaining the integrity and value of the piece. However, with more modern pieces of furniture it makes more sense to use up-to-date upholstery practices and materials, such as staples instead of tacks. Some of the more modern tools such as the staple gun have transformed the practice of upholstery, saving time and in some cases allowing for greater accuracy; however, the traditional methods remain a skill and art form in themselves. Different upholstery tools and materials and how to use them are also discussed.

The basic techniques section covers the practical side of upholstery, taking you through the fundamental techniques and also some of the more complex ones. The main section of the book – upholstered furniture – deals with how to reupholster a good cross section of different styles and types of furniture, focusing on techniques that are relevant to particular pieces, such as deep buttoning a late nineteenth-century chair and

The appeal of this Deco-style chair, left, lies in the simplicity of its lines and the combination of textures. The wooden arms have a wonderful shape and their hand-polished finish contrasts well with the matt texture of the soft leather upholstery.

Although the upholstery on this chair, right, needs to be completely rebuilt, the wooden frame is in good condition with well proportioned and elegant arms, making it well worth the time and effort to upholster.

how to apply double piping to a French chair. Cross references to other projects and the techniques section, as well as materials and tools, ensure that each project is easy to master.

If you are a beginner, start with the basic techniques, working your way up to more complex skills. Provide yourself with a workspace, or better still a dedicated workshop. You will find that creating the right environment to work in, with sufficient space, and having the appropriate tools readily available will help you enjoy the art of upholstery and improve your technique more quickly.

Patience, accuracy, and an eye for detail are vital

foundations of good upholstery. It is important to build a sound framework right from the beginning so that the finished piece is both sturdy and well made. Achieving the right shape and overall proportions is paramount. It should become a habit to continually stand back from your work to check the shapes you are forming are round and well balanced.

Take your time over each piece of furniture, appreciating the satisfaction of creating rolled edges and perfectly shaped mounds of padding. Imagine each chair, sofa, or stool as a work of art to which you are adding your own skill, detail, and interpretation. Each piece is an evolving landscape, enjoy!

tools, materials, and finishes

sourcing furniture

Whether you are looking for a specific style or piece of furniture or just waiting for something special to catch your eye, there is a great deal of choice – from curvaceous chaises longues to elegant club chairs, from original Arts and Crafts-styled chairs to exquisite wooden framed French chairs, from 1970s vintage furniture to petite footstools. Hunting out interesting pieces of furniture can be exciting and hugely rewarding. There is a variety of places to look for interesting furniture, including auction houses, local and international antique markets, junk shops, dedicated antique shops, and classified sections of specialist magazines and local newspapers and, of course, the Internet. This has a growing number of websites devoted to second hand and period furniture, specialist antique shops, and online auctions – the suppliers section at the back of the book details some helpful listings. Many auction houses now also have their forthcoming

stock listed and sometimes on view on their websites, a few days before the actual auction; this gives you an idea of what will be on sale, saving both time and energy, although ultimately seeing the piece in the flesh remains the best way to ascertain its worth and character.

When looking for a piece of furniture, consider first how you will be using it. For example, if it is a chair, will it be put to practical use as an every day item or is it intended for more decorative use and therefore not frequently used, such as the Arts and Crafts chair on page 84. Functionality versus practicality must be considered in all cases. All chairs are made for sitting on but differ in their uses and therefore in how they are constructed. If you are choosing something as a first upholstery project, it is a good idea to take this into account, perhaps starting with something simple. Dining chairs, salon chairs, and side chairs, for instance, are intended for relatively

These two 1920s club chairs, left, in orange vinyl with bun feet, have been well maintained over the years, but now both are in great need of revitalising.

An original deco chair, right, although requiring restoration work, reveals much potential in its overall shape and wooden arms and legs.

short stays only, which is reflected in their make-up — they have comparatively little in way of stuffing — whereas arm chairs, which are intended to be sat in for longer periods, are typically made with springs and a greater amount of stuffing thus making them a more complex project to work on.

Having found a piece of furniture that is appealing, consider its overall character, shape, and style. Does it have good, well-balanced proportions, is it open and generous, what, if any, is the detailing like, and is it comfortable? This is especially important with chairs: coming home to a chair is like coming home to a friend, it will always be there so it is important that you make the right choice. Next, take a look at the legs as these can greatly affect the look of a piece of furniture. Do they have well balanced, fine turnings, what kind of wood are they, are the back legs straight or elegantly splayed? If the chair has castors, are they original? Take time to study a piece of furniture before buying it, making sure that it is intact and of sound structure. Where possible, check that all

piece to a specialist restorer who can either make good any bad knocks or scratches, or strip the wood back to its natural state and repolish it by hand; the results can be very rewarding. The Deco chair on page 11 clearly needed work, especially as the join in one of the arms had become separated, however, it was still worth restoring. Once the arm was repaired with a near invisible join, all the wood was then stripped back and repolished by hand, giving an end result of a dark and rich finish. The chair back was reupholstered in a fine brown horsehair and the seat in brown suede, suede piping was used to define each of the three panels on the back and also around the front and side panels – the result was quite elegant and stunning.

The original 1930s leather chair on page 13 still had much character, the plain wooden arms complementing the leather and the row of studs accentuating the curve in the arms. During restoration the wooden arms were repolished, they developed a richer, more interesting patina and became a key feature of the chair. A soft tan leather, not dissimilar to the original was chosen to reupholster the chair, which in time would gain character. The elegant, late nineteenth-century balloon-back chair (left) showed great potential because its woodwork was so beautiful. The frame was quite fine and there were leaf carvings around the chair back and wonderfully shaped legs. A plain material was used in the upholstery – honey-coloured pony skin with a single line of antique finish studs – allowing the detail in the chair and the shape of the chair to become the main attraction.

The first impression of the club chairs (on page 10) was that they were rather crude in their plastic vinyl covering and large, outdated castors. However, their shape and proportions were appealing with simple, shaped front uprights and deep, generous seats. They were originally sold as a pair, one is in fact slightly smaller than the other as it is intended as a ladies chair while the other was made for a gentleman. The chairs were transformed by removing the old castors, polishing the bun feet, adding generous feather-filled cushions and reupholstering the chairs in a soft coffee-coloured brown leather with a suede covering in saddle stitch for the cushions.

When you obtain a piece of furniture, remember to ask for a receipt containing a brief description of the item, especially if you are a piece as an investment. Also, with items

the parts are original – do not be afraid to turn it upside down to examine the framework. Look for woodworm holes, if they are present, check to see whether the worm is still active (active holes may have small powder marks around them or powder may come out when you turn the item on its side and tap it). Avoid active woodworm. If you decide to buy a piece that has evidence of woodworm take it to a wood restorer for treatment. Make sure the whole frame is treated and not just the wood that can be seen.

The wood on a piece of furniture can contribute hugely to its character and is sometimes the main attraction. If the wood is in poor condition, for example if it has scratches or indent marks or has been painted over, consider taking the that are bought as investments, it is worth paying to have any scratches or broken parts mended professionally as this will help to retain the item's value. The age of a piece can often be seen in the wear and tear on the wood around the frame and on the legs. Sometimes, in peeling back the different layers of upholstery, you will also reveal something of its past, either in finding earlier, authentic and original fabrics or even discovering the original maker's mark or a serial number on the underside or back leg of a piece, thus adding to the authenticity and consequently the potential value of a piece.

Finding an interesting piece of furniture suitable for reupholstering can take time and effort, any potential may not always be immediately obvious but with inspiration it is amazing how a chair, sofa, or chaise longue can be brought back to life with the most rewarding results. Patience, imagination, and a good eye for detail will take you far. . .

This elegant 19th century balloon-backed dining chair, left, required only plain covering to bring out the fine detail in the wood and shape of the chair back and legs.

With this original 1930s leather chair, right, simply re-upholstering the chair in soft tan leather and restoring the wood provided it with a new lease of life.

tools

Relatively few tools are needed to get started in upholstery. The main items that you will need include a magnetic hammer, a ripping chisel, a wood mallet, a web strainer, a tack lifter, and a good pair of scissors. As you refine your working methods over time, these will gradually be augumented and personalized with other items that you find useful.

The tools you use are key to how you work as they will gradually become an extension of your hands, finely tuned to your rhythm. It is worthwhile searching for good quality tools that have been made for professionals, as these will have been designed specifically to help you work with the greatest of ease.

This section includes those tools that are suitable for more traditional upholstery techniques, such as a magnetic hammer and tacks, as well as the more modern implements of the trade, such as a staple gun. The age and design of a piece of furniture, and how much time you have available, will influence the tools you prefer to use. For example, when working on a

1	**hide strainer**	This is used to manipulate leather but can it can also be used as a web strainer, holding the webbing and pulling it into place.
2	**web strainer – conventional wooden strainer**	Used to achieve tension when securing a strip of webbing, this is an important tool and key in creating a good base of webbing on which to build the subsequent layers of material.
3	**magnetic hammer**	Very handy when applying tacks, a magnetic hammer enables you to pick up and position a tack with one hand, leaving your other hand free to hold the fabric. Using this tool takes a little practice but is worth the effort.
4	**cabriole hammer**	This hammer has a smaller tip than a magnetic hammer, and is used for more delicate areas and around show wood (the wood that will be visible).
5	**mallet**	A wooden mallet is used in conjuction with the ripping chisel (**9**) to remove old tacks. Different sizes are available so choose one that you find easy to use.
6	**scissors**	A small pair of scissors is useful for reaching inaccessible places and shaping fabric, while a large pair is good for cutting large pieces of fabric such as top fabric, hessian, and calico.
7	**pincers**	Pincers are good for encouraging stubborn tacks and staples to come out.
8	**pliers with wire cutters**	Helpful when trying to take out old staples, wire cutters cut into the staple which can then be pulled out with pliers.
9	**ripping chisel**	Very handy for removing tacks, this is used in conjuction with the mallet. The v-shape at the end fits under the tack. Angled or straight blades are available.
10	**tack lifter**	This has a small v-shape at the end which helps to extract tacks.
11	**staple puller**	The shaped end of the staple puller is used specifically for extracting staples but at times it is also helpful for extracting tacks.
12	**craft knife**	Useful for trimming away fabric. Make sure the blade is always sharp.
13	**bradawl**	This has a pointed end that is good for making holes or marks.
14	**staple gun**	Used more often now than the traditional hammer and tacks as it is quicker and more precise. Staple guns that work from an air compressor (**a**) are more powerful, however electric and non-powered varieties (**b**) are also effective.

delicate part of a chair or around an area that is difficult to access, it makes more sense to use a staple gun than a hammer and tacks.

A sewing machine is a very useful tool for upholstery. Most modern machines intended for domestic sewing can be used. However, with some materials, such as leather or hide, it is advisable to take marked-up panels to someone who has an industrial machine that can cope with them, such as a commercial upholsterer or local seamstress.

Aim to have all your tools readily accessible and somewhere they can easily be located. A well-organized area dedicated to your upholstery will be invaluable and will help you to work efficiently. Give yourself as much space as possible and find a good size workbench – a large surface will be needed to lay out and cut the lengths of fabric. If you do not have a workbench or table that you can leave in place, use a pair of trestles with a piece of plywood, or similar, over the top. Make sure you have sufficient light to work in as you will need to be precise and accurate. If the overhead light is not strong enough then find a desk light that can be angled to focus on whatever area you are working on. Providing yourself with the right environment will help you enjoy your upholstery.

1 sewing machine feet	**a** Double grooved foot for making double piping.	
	b Flat foot for zips and plain seams.	
	c Single, slim grooved piping foot for making fine single piping.	
	d Single grooved piping foot for making single piping.	
2 bobbin	Holds the backing thread on a sewing machine.	
3 sewing machine needles	These range in size and type, and can be more sharply pointed than other needles.	
4 glue sticks	Used in conjunction with a hot-glue gun.	
5 glue gun	Used mainly for attaching trimmings around a frame. The sticks melt and hot glue is released as the trigger is pulled in.	
6 double-ended needle	A needle with a point at each end, used for roll stitch, wall stitch, and through stitching.	
7 circular needle	A semi-circular needle used for slip stitching.	
8 upholstery pins	Strong steel pins used for holding fabric in place, available in different sizes.	
9 regulator	A very useful tool, used mainly to manipulate stuffing into place. Also comes in handy in a number of different ways, including holding fabric in place and accessing difficult to reach areas. Available with or without a wooden handle.	
10 retractable measure	Steel measure, good for measuring large pieces of fabric.	
11 tape measure	A loose measuring tape is helpful for measuring round shapes.	
12 wood rule	Useful when cutting fabric on a flat surface and for drawing straight lines on fabric.	
13 skewers	Used for pinning and holding fabric and pleats in place, offering a stronger hold than normal pins; available in different sizes.	
14 spring needle	A gently curved needle used for attaching springs to webbing and hessian.	
15 tailor's chalk	Used to mark up fabric. Where possible always use on the reverse side of fabric.	
set square (not shown)	Good for achieving 90 degree angles.	
spray adhesive (not shown)	Contact adhesive in aerosol form useful for attaching foam to board.	

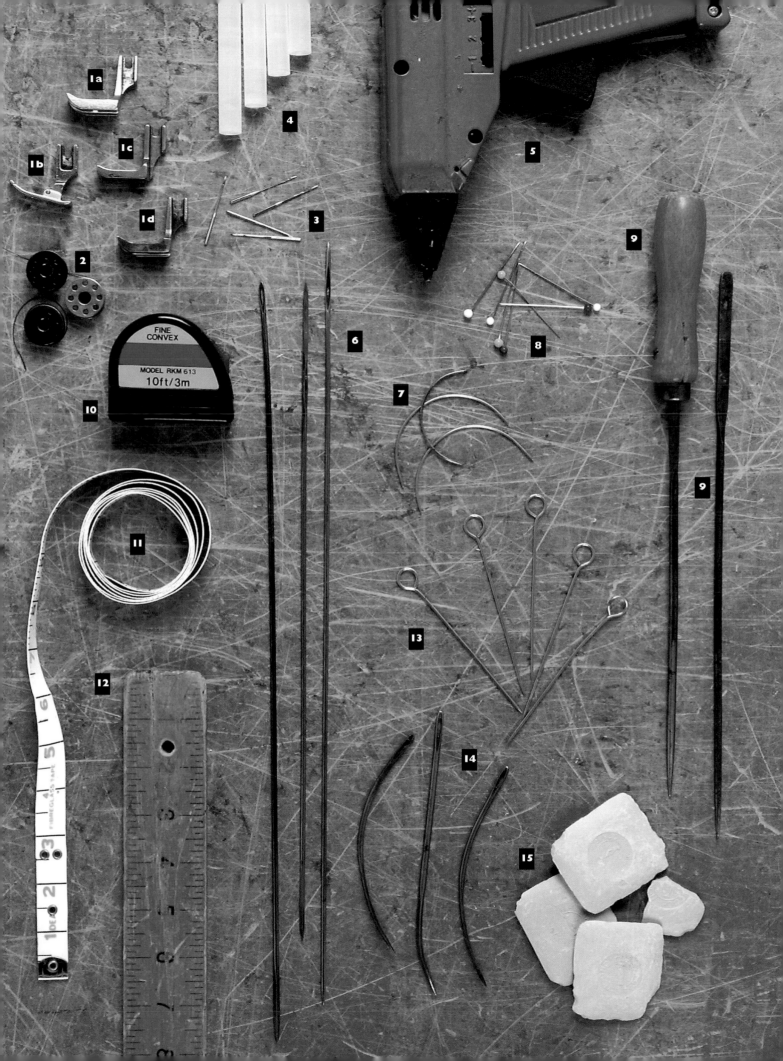

upholstery materials

There are several standard materials used throughout upholstery, each with
their own specific role to play. The majority of them come in a variety of
widths and thicknesses, depending upon the use for which they are
intended. As with tools, acquiring good quality materials is paramount; they
will ensure that a piece of furniture is well constructed, and capable of
being used for its intended purpose, without falling apart. Often the
materials are only sold in bulk so it may be worthwhile buying quantities
with fellow students or friends. Be sure to order on the generous side,
rather than risk running out. Some specialist upholstery shops cater for
people who want smaller quantities, other suppliers have mail order
catalogues and will dispatch the materials in the post or by courier. If you
are having difficulty locating a supplier, try asking a local upholsterer who
may be happy to place an order for you alongside his own.

Even though each type of material has a specific use, over time, you will
work out which materials you prefer for different jobs. For example, for

1	polyester wadding	Manmade fibre that looks like white candyfloss or cotton candy. This is used between calico and the top fabric in modern upholstery, and is also sometimes used for wrapping foam. 55g (2oz), 110g (4oz), and 250g (9oz) are the most common weights used.
2	hessian	Looking somewhat similar to sack cloth, this is made of jute and is used to hold stuffing in place. Different weights and widths are available; the most commonly used weight is 285g (10oz).
3	barrier cloth	Similar in texture to calico, this has built-in fire-retardant properties and, in some cases, can be used in place of calico to meet fire regulations.
4	black fibre	A modern, fire-retardant substitute for horsehair.
5	calico	A strong cotton fabric used to cover the padding on a chair beneath the final fabric.
6	lining cloth	Used to cover a seat when a padded cushion is part of the chair. Choose a colour that complements the top fabric you are using, otherwise an offcut of top fabric can be used instead.
7	skin wadding	Two layers of "skin" holding in a fluffy cotton centre. This acts as a barrier under top fabric helping to stop it slipping. It comes in different weights, the most commonly used is 1700g (48oz).
8	dust cloth	Used to cover the underside of a chair, creating a neat finish. Hessian is sometimes used in place of a dust cloth.
9	cotton felt	This looks like rough cottonwool and is used where minimal padding is needed. It also helps create the final shape and provides padding before the top fabric is applied. It can be used in place of wadding, typically under calico. Used more frequently in traditional upholstery.
	horsehair (not shown)	This stuffing was used in traditional upholstery but is now difficult and expensive to obtain. However, old horsehair can be washed and reused (see page 41, step 5).
	foam (not shown)	Foam can be used instead of feather stuffing for seat cushions and is now used widely in modern upholstery.

some jobs you may prefer to use a thick material, while for others, thinner layers are more versatile as they can be built up gradually to create the desired thickness. Tacks come in a wide range of sizes. Not only are they available in different lengths but each length also has two sizes of tack head: one fine, the other "improved". The fine head is intended for more delicate jobs, and improved is used where greater strength is required, such as webbing. Again, you will soon learn which you prefer to use for what job; this will also be influenced by the age and condition of a chair and the style of top fabric you have chosen.

Traditionally, horsehair was used for stuffing and still remains the best material for stuffing today. However, it is now relatively difficult to acquire and also expensive. The alternative is a manmade black fibre. When you are working on a period piece of furniture that you wish to upholster using traditional methods, it is important to try and use horsehair to maintain the integrity of the piece. Often the old horsehair can be reused by washing it either by hand or in a washing machine secured firmly within an old pillowcase or such like.

1 zig zag springs	Used more in modern furniture, these can be attached to the seat or back of a chair.
2 double cone springs	Used in traditional upholstery, these come in various sizes, the lower the gauge, the thicker and, therefore, the stronger the spring. The more typical sizes used for seats are gauge 8 or 9, for backs gauge 10, and for arms gauge 12 or 13.
3 webbing	**a** Black and white "English" herringbone webbing is the strongest.
	b Brown jute webbing is the most commonly used.
	c Elasticated webbing is used on seats and chair backs for a strong base for seat cushions.
	Each of these are sold in 5cm (2in) widths, on the roll.
4 gimp pins	Small, fine pins with a small head used to hold gimp and braid in place and in places where a discreet fixing is needed. They can also be used in place of tacks if a smaller tack is needed. They come in a variety of colours.
5 tacks	Used in traditional upholstery, there are two types: fine with a small head and "improved" with a larger head. They also come in different sizes. Typically, 10mm (⅜in) tacks are used for hessian and calico, and 13mm (½in) tacks are used for webbing and top fabric.
6 studs	Used as decorative nails to hold leather and fabric in place (see pages 34–5).
7 zip	Used for cushion covers.
8 slipping thread	Used to hand-stitch two pieces of fabric together, this comes in a variety of colours to match the top fabric.
9 sewing machine thread	Usually polyester cotton, available in different colours and strengths.
10 stitching twine	Also known as upholstery twine, this is used for stuffing ties, through stitching, and bridle ties.
11 buttoning twine	A strong nylon cord used to tie off deep buttons.
12 piping cord	White cotton cord, used for single and double piping. It comes in different widths, typically No 1 gauge is used.
13 laid cord	A strong cord used for lashing springs to hold them in place. Made of hemp or jute.
staples (not shown)	Used in staple guns in modern upholstery. In some cases, staples offer a neater finish, and are easier to use on more delicate areas. They come in different sizes, the most commonly used are 10mm (⅜in) and 14mm (⅝in).
back tacking strip (not shown)	A strip of card used to create a neat, straight edge in top fabric along a tack line.

fabrics

Selecting a fabric to upholster a chair, sofa, or any other item is no mean feat these days as there is such a wealth from which to choose. Begin by considering the character of the piece of furniture, what you like about it, what sort of fabric it is upholstered in now, and how you might like to bring it to life. This is not always an immediate process, particularly if you have only recently acquired it; if this is the case, live with it in situ for a while so you can get a better idea of what would suit it. Think about its shape. Is it elegant, decorative, chunky, petite, elaborate, tall? Is the show wood quite special and, therefore, only in need of a plain fabric such as linen to enhance it, or if there is no show wood, is the shape of the chair interesting enough that, again, a plain fabric will work well? Alternatively, if the piece is pleasing because of its simplicity, would a textured or patterned fabric help to accentuate this? A plain fabric allows for finer detail and interest to be added through the trimming or finishing work: studs, ribbon, or piping, for example. The use of plain double piping on a plain fabric on page 110 creates a subtle effect that works well because it gently accentuates the contours of the wood.

Next, think about how often the piece of furniture will be used. If it is a chair, will it be sat on everyday or just occasionally, perhaps being more for decoration than practical use? If it is going to be used fairly frequently, then a fabric that will allow for wear and tear will be more appropriate than a delicate silk or suede. The reverse side of a swatch or sample will have details of the purposes the fabric is suitable for; if you are unsure what the references mean ask your supplier. Most fabrics also have a rub test reference; the higher the rub reference, the more durable the fabric will be. It is very important you check with the suppplier the fabric you wish to use meets the relevant fire and safety standards. Some fabrics are inherently fire retardant, others which are not can be used with a fire retardant barrier cloth or can be back-coated to meet these regulations. In some cases, if a piece of furniture is pre-1950s, the FR standards differ and are sometimes more lenient. Fabrics featured in this book include those that are suitable for upholstery, as well as those that are suitable for cushions and more decorative purposes. Some fabric types,

such as alcantara (faux suede), typically have high endurance and are easily cleaned, while others, such as silk, are more easily damaged and difficult to clean. This need not be a problem as there are companies who will come to your home and dry clean a piece of furniture, but again, check with your supplier to make sure this is a suitable treatment for your particular fabric.

Once you have decided on the type of fabric you would like to use, you need to consider its texture (pages 24–5),

The combination of plain linen with bold velvet stripes, left, will create a striking impact on any piece, whilst the fabric on the right will create a more subtle effect, using three different shades of red in suede, satin, and silk.

colour (pages 26–7), and, if it has any, its pattern (pages 28–9). Think about all these in reference to the item itself and also the space in which it will sit. Factors such as whether it will be under natural or artificial light, in a bright room or a dark one or one with plenty of shadows, in ornate surroundings or in a fairly plain space will all have an impact on the way the fabric looks. For example, light on velvet excentuates the curves and shadows, creating a sensuous feel, while those of a lighter nature, such as silk, will reflect the light.

Once you have a good idea of what you want, start the search. If possible, visit more than one fabric supplier as each will stock fabric by different designers and you will get a better feel for what is available, as well as a greater choice. When you find something you like, be prepared to ask for samples – often these can be given on the spot or will be sent to you: do not be afraid to ask for several. In addition to smaller samples, it is also possible to obtain larger pieces, usually 50cm (20in) or 1m (40in) in size. These are great for draping over the piece of furniture and leaving in place for a couple of weeks so you can be sure you are happy with your choice. It is not easy to imagine how a piece of furniture will look with its new fabric but intuition will go a long way. Do not be afraid of choosing a fabric that is quite different or dramatic – the results can be highly satisfying.

this cotton/viscose mix (Strata from Sahco Hesslein) produces a wonderful, ridged texture. To balance the ridges running from side to side, the fabric is punctuated by darker and lighter shades of the same colour lengthwise. This creates a subtle but very interesting effect, and when used on a simple shape (such as the chair opposite) has a stunning impact.

this polyester material (Taffeta Pleat from Kravet) is perfect where a very sumptuous effect is required. The intricate pleating produces light and shade in between each minute fold and is reminiscent of the gills on the underside of a mushroom. This fabric would work very well in conjunction with a plain fabric in a similar colour shade.

pony skin is available in attractive natural colours, such as honey and mushroom-brown, and is a very soft tactile material. It is striking beside rich show wood or with other materials, such as suede. With every day use it can wear relatively fast so it is best used on cushions and occasional seating. You may need to buy it through an upholsterer; always check that it is a by-product.

leather is in fashion once more. There are many types to choose from varying in colour, feel, and quality. Good quality leather is soft to the touch and quite pliable. Heavily processed leather is more durable but may not be such a good texture. For a leather that will age and gain character quickly, choose aniline types. Leather is typically sold by the whole hide.

horsehair (this is Gotland from John Boyd Textiles) is available in a host of different colours and patterns. It is also possible to have your own design made up. Horsehair can be quite striking and is excellent for creating a glamorous ambience. It comes in relatively short widths so careful consideration needs to be taken when estimating how much is needed for a piece of furniture.

suede, like leather, is once again in vogue. It is another very tactile material, soft and luxurious to the touch. Different sizes and thicknesses of suede are available, along with a great variety of colours. If the suede is relatively thin then it can often be sewn on a household sewing machine. However, if it is quite thick, it may need to be taken to an upholsterer.

texture

Due to ever-evolving technology the choice of different fabric textures continues to grow. Only a small selection of the huge number is illustrated here. While some fabrics may consist of all natural fibres, such as wool, cotton, or silk, they are now also combined with other materials, often manmade, thus opening the door to a greater variety of finishes. Fabrics with a combination of textures, such as the linen and velvet stripe on page 22, are also offered. Other unusual textures that are now widely available include those created with metallic threads. Again, there is a dazzling assortment to choose from, each offering a different effect. Some fabrics with more elaborate and innovative textures, such as rubber coatings or those with a large metallic content, can be difficult to imagine upholstered on a piece of furniture, and initially they will take some courage to use, but with practice, you will find that you gain confidence about what will look good and it is possible to create quite stunning pieces.

To a great extent, the style of the piece of furniture to be covered – its age, shape, and character – will dictate the types

this faux suede, which is sometimes called alcantara, closely resembles suede in its look and feel. In most cases this type of fabric is very durable and easily cleaned. There is a wide choice of colours and qualities, some are much finer than others. This sample (Novasuede from Mary Fox Linton) has a wonderful feel and is of a high standard.

this wool fabric (Elepunto from Sahco Hesslein) has rows of perforated holes, in a twist to an otherwise plain look. The holes offer the opportunity to create a second dimension of interest as another fabric can be used underneath, either in a contrasting or similar colour. This type of fabric is not suitable for furniture that will be used on a daily basis.

this cotton/viscose mix (Kabuki Velvet from Conran), although a plain fabric, has a velvety luxurious feel to it. It would work well on a large comfortable chair or sofa with big cushions to sink into. However, it is a relatively thick fabric, so is less appropriate for a small chair with more delicate detailing.

linen lends a modern air to any piece of furniture. This linen (Gweneth Linen from Turnell & Gigon) has a good texture – not too grainy and not too thin. Of the myriad linens available, the slightly thicker types with some variation in the weave are most interesting in effect. The subtle texture of plain-coloured linens such as this looks great beside show wood (see the chair on page 110).

this faux fur (20911 from Kravet) is a particularly fine example that has great depth, warmth, and subtlety in colour and a wonderfully soft, opulent feel. In combination with a plain fabric, it works extremely well (see page 98, where it is also used to pick out the colours in the ovaltine-coloured wool). There are many imitation furs on the market, but few have such a rich look and feel.

a plain wool fabric (here Elemento from Sacho Hesslein) is highly versatile. Its matt finish is equally good on a fine piece of furniture, such as the button-back chair on page 98, as it is on a plain, more contemporary style of furniture. Its simplicity makes it suitable for combining with many other fabrics, including leather, suede, and faux fur.

of textures that will be appropriate. For example, a fabric with a contemporary-style thick pile will probably not sit well on a petite refined antique chair. A variety of very obvious textures on one piece of furniture will have the effect of looking cluttered and crude, while two or three textures carefully chosen to complement each other will produce subtle and interesting results; for instance leather, suede, and velvet are often excellent together.

With textured fabrics it is important to consider where an item will be displayed as the amount and type of light it is exposed to will have a considerable effect. Some fabrics, such as those with a deep pile or with a thicker weave like wool, have a matt appearance, while silk and rubberized fabrics tend to reflect light. A fabric with a textured metallic stripe is good for emphasizing the line of chair, as is velvet, which highlights sensuous curves, of chair arms or backs for instance.

Some textured fabrics are prone to wear, so make sure the type you choose is appropriate for the use it will receive – check with your supplier if you are not sure.

this linen (Woodstock Stone from Andrew Martin) catches the light in a subtle way that is very effective alongside rich show wood (see page 110). The neutral tones are offset by the dark polish on the wood, while the dark background has the effect of making the fabric look relatively pale. This tone also complements brighter colours such as those on page 146.

reminiscent of the colour of field mushrooms, the tone of this fabric (Fiji from Sacho Hesslein) is very warm. Although the colour is relatively strong, it would combine well with others. The warm appearance of the fabric is enhanced by it being rather soft and tactile.

although this fabric (Lavello from Sacho Hesslein) is basically cream, it has a hint of pink that produces a warmer tone and makes it more interesting, especially as its surface also has a slight sheen. Such gentle colouring works well in many settings and combinations without any sense of it being invasive.

this is a good example of how a rather plain fabric (9206 863 Etamine from Zimmer & Rhode) can still be very appealing. The colour tone is relatively warm and light and would combine well with a number of different hues, being equally effective with oatmeal or cream colours as well as more earthy browns.

of the many chocolate brown fabrics on the market, some are too dark and others are too orangey brown. This velvet (Lafayette from Manuel Canovas) is a very rich example, really reminiscent of cocoa. It succeeds because its hue is natural, and its texture means it will work well on furniture with soft curves and shapes, showing shadow and light. However, it will tend to absorb light too.

this again is quite a plain coloured fabric (Alpaca from Sacho Hesslein), similar in colour to the worn rounded pebbles found on a beach. Because it is a light colour, it is relatively versatile, blending particularly well with other pebble- or stone-coloured fabrics.

colour

Colour is often the first consideration when choosing fabric for a piece of furniture. It has the potential for a more immediate impact than the texture and, sometimes, the pattern, too. Evolved colour creation and dying methods in the fabric industry mean there are now a great many subtleties in any one colour, creating a huge spectrum of shades from which to choose. Be prepared to take time to find just the right one.

It is difficult to do justice to all the colours available so we have focused on neutral tones and some of the more interesting shades of key colours to give an idea of the variety of choice. Neutral colours are continually desirable and have a number of interpretations. For example, with any two shades of "stone" or "cream", (such as "Woodstock" and "Lavello" on the left), there can be a vast difference in effect; in the two shown, one has a lighter pinker hue, making it warmer, while the other is cooler, with a very slight hint of grey.

As with texture, light has an immense impact on the colour of a fabric. Typically, dark colours absorb light and lighter colours reflect it. A colour can very often look

both rich and interesting, this crab-apple red fabric (1881944 from Kravet) has an intriguing effect on the light, which means it would look good on a button-back chair or one with plenty of curves. There are many shades of red to choose from, so it should not be difficult to find exactly the shade you require.

this fabric (Lafayette from Colefax & Fowler) has an almost smoky hue. It is a wonderful example of how colours are evolving and becoming more versatile. The overall impact of this colour is quite subtle, with an earthy undertone.

reminiscent of raspberry ripples and cassis, the rich pink colour of this fabric (Fiesole from Designers Guild) has a smoky quality that gives it more depth than many other shades of pink.

another fabulous colour, this blue fabric (Lafayette from Colefax & Fowler) is interesting because of its depth and richness. It is a shade that is both strong and vibrant.

one of the more special shades of blue, this fabric (Lafayette from Colefax & Fowler), is a subtle blend of duck-egg blue and French blue. It immediately stands out from other blues because it is quite unusual in tone.

this icy lime-green fabric (Tizian from JAB) is appealing because it is vibrant and contemporary, while somehow being soft and soothing too. It is effective against metallic surfaces, such as aluminium (see page 138), and is complemented by richer, darker shades of green. It also works well when combined with a neutral background, such as plain linen (see page 146).

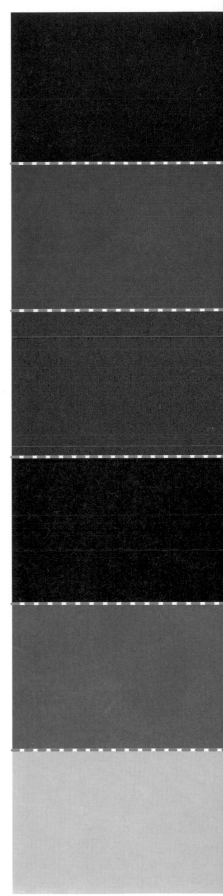

completely different under natural light and artificial light, so bear in mind the planned setting for your piece – will it be next to a big window or by a tall lamp, for example? Make sure you look at a piece of fabric in daylight before deciding whether it is the right shade.

Take care to consider all the other colours in the room, not only the other pieces of furniture but also the carpet or floor covering and the walls. The colours do not have to be the same, but if you decide on a contrast or a complementary tone, it is important to get it right. Combining different shades of the same colour can be very effective, although this takes time and a good eye. When you go to choose fabric, if possible take samples of the other fabrics in the room with you. Alternatively, take several samples of different shades home from the retailer before you make a purchase. Hold the swatches of fabric against each of the other items in the room to be sure that the colours work well together. If you are introducing a very different colour, try living for a week or two with a large swatch of the proposed fabric draped over the relevant item to see whether it will really work or not.

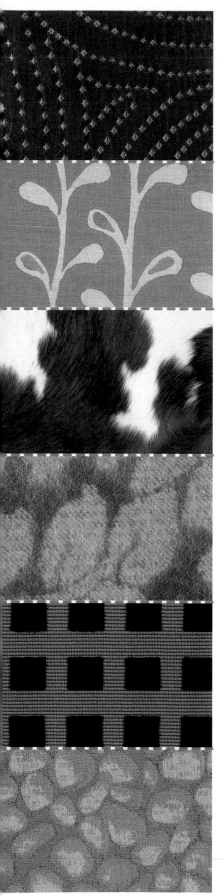

sometimes a very simple pattern can have great effect; the small gold threads of this fabric (Ice Dance from Mulberry) give a wonderful feeling of movement. It can be effective in picking out a similar colour gold in the wood of a piece of furniture or following its swirls and curves (see page 150). Further interest is added when the gold thread catches the light.

this fabric (Sweet Pea from Nina Campbell) has an unusual design that is block printed by hand. Combined with the contemporary colour chosen for the background, the overall effect of the pattern is quite striking. It would work well in a variety of different spaces.

using cowhide for upholstery is increasingly popular. The effect is both tactile and distinctive. Hide is best used in large pieces to gain the benefit of the whole pattern (see page 134) rather than in patches of smaller pieces. It also works effectively as a cushion for a leather chair, breaking up the monotony of the leather. Ensure that the hide is a by-product.

this fabric (Windfall from Larsen) has a relatively strong pattern and would work well on a chair with a simple frame. The warm earthy colours suit the naturalistic character of the print.

the square lines of this fabric (89361-973 from Brunschwig & Fils) are set off by the subtle black and gold stripe in the background. This lighter colouring does much to enhance the small squares, which are in a rich, sumptuous, black velvet flock. The overall effect is quite stunning, grand, and contemporary. A similar pattern (without flock) has been used on the chair, right.

this fabric (Pebbles from Mulberry) is composed of four different tones, giving it depth and enhancing the shadow effect on the "pebbles". This is an excellent example of a pattern that could be used to bring out the character of a chair, while somehow also remaining subtle in how it achieves this – for example an old French chair painted in similar colours.

pattern

Using a patterned fabric can have a considerable impact on the look and feel of a piece of furniture. There are many, many different pattern types and sizes available and visualizing what a patterned fabric might look like on a piece of furniture can be difficult. Factors to consider include choosing a suitable scale of pattern for the size of the piece: the pattern shouldn't swamp the item but should sit comfortably on all the different parts without being chopped up beyond recognition or compromised in any other way. Consider too, the shape of the piece and the shape of the pattern; for example, a pattern with a circular motif may work well on a chair with curves, such as sweeping or rounded arms. A piece with strong geometry will also look good covered with a fabric that has complementary or contrasting shapes in it (see the Arts and Crafts easy chair on page 90, for example).

Also important is whether the pattern you choose will blend with or enhance other patterns in the same room; patterns can and do work together but it takes a discerning eye and experience to get it right. As with colours, if possible it is best to have a large sample of the fabric at home for a

week or so, draped over the piece of furniture for which it is intended, so that you can be sure you have chosen the right one. A fabric with a small pattern will have a relatively subtle impact in a room as the effect of the pattern will be diminished, especially viewed from a distance. On the other hand, a fabric with a large pattern can dictate the whole style of the space. Using a large design is a bold step, but it can be very rewarding, creating a strong statement in a room or enhancing the natural character of a piece of furniture. For example, the striped fabric used on the wing chair on page 114, brings to life the architecture of the chair, the strong lines of the pattern accentuating the slim, straight arms, back, and wings. Although it is an antique, the contemporary feel of the fabric gives the chair a new lease of life.

A patterned fabric becomes even more interesting when it also has a variety of textures (such as the fabric with black velvet squares, page 28). This has the effect of increasing the sense of depth and the overall impact.

It may take time to find exactly what you want for your furniture, however, once you have made a decision, it is very exciting watching the transformation take place. Making a choice with confidence can have very positive results.

this striking pattern (Cordellina from Designers Guild) is made effective by the vibrant colours and strong stripes. It is further enriched by the raised flock, which gives added depth. A very contemporary style of fabric, this would be particularly attractive on a piece of furniture with a simple linear structure. The variety of colours makes it easy to combine with other similarly coloured fabrics.

this geometric pattern (Melanie from Anna French) has great impact, immediately bringing an Art Deco character to a room or space. The rich and interesting colours that have been used really enhance the pattern, their impact offset by the individual, non-perfect shapes, which soften the whole look.

the wide stripe on this fabric (Step 1 from Mary Fox Linton) creates an air of extravagance and glamour. Although a very simple pattern, it makes a strong impression that is softened by the subtle colours. Used on a bold but simply shaped piece of furniture the effect of this fabric would be quite stunning.

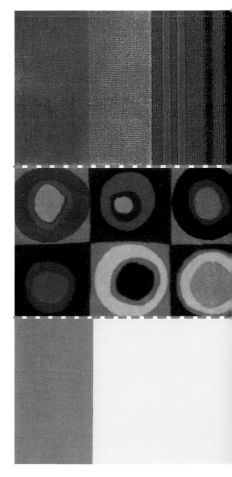

both of these fabrics are visually strong, offering opportunities for a striking combination. The velvet (Otello from Mary Fox Linton) is a deep midnight-black and the pewter-coloured polyester fabric (Meteorite from Kravet) has an unusual but pleasingly smooth feel. Two fabrics such as these would be effective on a piece of furniture with curves, giving depth and creating shadow, which would accentuate shapes in the light. Apart from the different textures working well together – one soft and sumptuous, the other matt with a rubber-type finish – the colours also combine well: the black velvet picks out the black that is engrained in the shades of pewter and silver in the polyester.

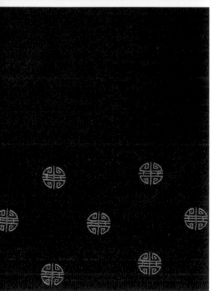

these two fabrics work well together because they are so different, one is very plain and the other has a strong but delicate pattern, it is their colours that unite them. The rich deep red velvet (18844 from Kravet) has a very opulent feel and is potentially quite heavy in appearance, however the gold symbols on the dupioni silk (21909–9 also from Kravet) lighten the effect and offer relief and interest. The silk also brings another dimension with its hint of Asia. The red thread in the dupioni silk is not dissimilar to that in the velvet; both are enhanced by the light, producing interesting shadows.

this lambswool and cashmere fabric (Alexi from George Spencer) has a herringbone pattern in subtle shades of pale green, grey, and cream. The fabric is very soft to the touch and would create a luxurious feel on any piece of furniture. In contrast to this, the satin (Satin Latour from Turnell & Gigon) is very plain, but it offers relief to the herringbone weave, with the colour picking up the lighter shade in the herringbone. This is another luxurious fabric. The two fabrics also work well together because the wool has a matt finish and the satin, a subtle but wonderful sheen.

combining fabrics

The different characteristics that make up a fabric – the texture, weave, colour, and pattern – come together to offer opportunities for an amazing and never-ending variety of combinations. When selecting a fabric, or fabrics, remember to take into consideration other aspects that will influence the finished piece, such as the trimming and the cushions. All these will influence your choice; when combined successfully, they will become extensions of the main body of fabric.

Depth and interest can be produced simply by using one colour in materials of different textures. For example, the base of a sofa might be upholstered in a warm pebble-coloured leather with scatter cushions in suede with saddle stitch detail and other cushions that are in stone-coloured pony skin with suede backs. Or, a chair covered in chocolate-brown velvet would look wonderful with cushions covered in a similar chocolate-brown but in silk; the fact that these two textures

the natural fibres – silk, wool, and cotton – in each of these fabrics (right) combine effectively, with the colours in the patterned fabric (Orbit from George Spencer) uniting all three pieces. Although the fibres are natural, their textures are quite different; the wool and silk weave of the top fabric gives the most textured feel, while the combined silk and cotton in the brown satin (Satin Latour from Turnell & Gigon) gives a gentle sheen, and the plain duck-egg blue silk (Ardecia from Zimmer & Rhode) has a matt finish. The overall appearance of the combination is elegant, subtle, and interesting.

will reflect the light in different ways adds another dimension. Another way to create additional interest might be to use the same colour silk for a set of cushions but to upholster one with saddle stitch detail and another with tiny pleats; in this case, the effect will be quite sumptuous but very subtle (an example of pleated silk-type polyester can be seen on page 24: Taffeta Pleat from Kravet). Contrast can also be created by choosing a plain, matt fabric used against polished show wood; the two counter balance each other very effectively. Or, you could try brown leather contrasted with a luxurious brown, white, and black cowhide cushion, or cover the seat cushion of a leather chair with suede or velvet.

Some items of furniture offer the opportunity to combine fabrics in a slightly different way. For example, a pair of Victorian salon chairs with padded seats and round, padded backs framed in wood will often also have a panel of fabric on the outside back also framed by the show wood; for a subtle effect, this back panel could be upholstered in a fabric in the same shade but another texture.

Do not be afraid to explore, experiment, and be different. With so many choices available it is easy to create an individual look, something perhaps not so conventional.

this combination has a wonderful, harmonious feel. The colours work well together as the shades are similar but they are varied enough to provide interest and each of the fabrics has a very different texture. The top piece, the base fabric (Adara from Jewel), is very soft with a velvet-type weave. Something like this would be wonderful on a sofa or chair that has large curved arms as it catches the light, accentuating the shapes. To complement this, the two other fabrics (Tidepool and Dunes from Sahco Hesslein) add a subtle decorative touch. The background shade of the patterned fabric (Tidepool) is very close to that of the bottom fabric and so the tones work well; the swirls add relief to the two plain fabrics.

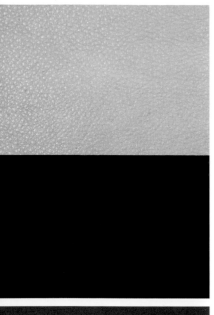

this pebble-coloured leather (Elmosoft Rustical from Elmo) looks very attractive set against a contrasting colour, in this case chocolate-brown. The very different textures work well together, the soft, smooth surface of the leather contrasting with the thick soft fur of the goat skin (Walter Reginald).

as a base fabric, the patterned linen (Iko from Colefax & Fowler) offers the opportunity to use complementary colours to bring out the tones in its stripes of beige, yellow, green, and purple. Instead of matching the velvet stripes exactly, a lighter green and a darker purple are chosen, complementing the base fabric but offering a slightly different twist. The plain, neutral look of the linen offers contrast and complements the richness of the velvets (Lafayette from Colefax & Fowler). Adding a final dimension is the lilac shade of velvet (Aladin from Conran), which picks up exactly the lilac stripe in the linen.

When you are considering combinations, try to imagine what the overall effect of a grouping of fabrics will be. Think about how the patterns, colours, and different textures will work together. Do not be tempted to overdo it, however, if too many effects are thrown together, then the overall impression may be rather overwhelming.

Remember, subtlety is often the key to success. The reason why a piece of furniture looks interesting or why a combination of fabrics works well does not necessarily have to be immediately obvious; in fact it is often more interesting when something is gradually revealed. Work at achieving an effective balance, ensuring there is a harmony with your

this group of smooth, supple leather (Barolo from JMT Leather), soft suede (a calf split from Walter Reginald), and rich velvet, (14743 from Kravet), works wonderfully well. All in similar shades of brown, the very plain but different textures produce a subtle winning combination. Often, when leather is used to upholster a piece of furniture, particularly when it is in a dark shade, the impact can be heavy and imposing; but, by adding a suede cushion or upholstering the seat in velvet, the impact can be lightened, making the piece more interesting. Alternatively, the outer arms or outside back of a chair can be upholstered in suede with the rest of the chair in leather.

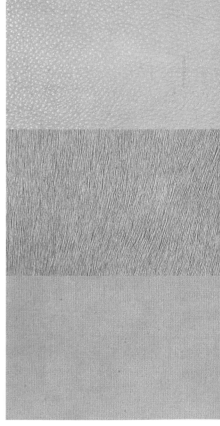

each of these three materials have very different textures; this, along with the subtle differences in colour, is the secret of their success. The leather (Elmosoft Rustical from Elmo) is very supple and smooth to the touch, the pony skin (natural pony skin from J T Batchelor) is soft to stroke but clearly has a very different texture, and the velvet (Aladin from Conran) has a thick pile. A spectacular use of this combination would be on a contemporary sofa: the leather for the main upholstery, the seat and back cushions in velvet, and scatter cushions in pony skin with suede backs to complement the arrangement.

ultimate choice of fabrics. Sometimes contrasts can be very striking while also being sophisticated and subtle. The sofa and stool above show how three different fabrics can be combined with great success. Here there are two base colours, which are then matched together in the striped fabric. The overall effect is bold and highly stylized. Integrating the patterned fabric not only on the decorative cushion, but also on the stool and the curtains is extremely effective. By using the stripe vertically as well as horizontally, the interest is heightened even more. The linear effect/theme is taken further by the simple, straight lines of the sofa and stool, and the vertical block of the screen in the background.

double piping These trimmings (31168 from Wemyss Houlès, top, and IF 4801/876 from Turnell & Gigon, bottom) are ready-made lengths of double piping. The rich claret-red would complement a patterned or textured top fabric, while the combination of sage- and lime-green, might work well with a plain fabric, discreetly adding interest. Double piping is excellent for accentuating the curves of a piece of furniture and for creating a clean, neat, and subtle finish.

single piping Single piping may be attached directly to the panels of fabric before both are secured to the piece of furniture, or it can be applied over the edge of a panel of fabric directly onto the item. These striking lengths of piping are in soft red leather (leather piping 28 from Altiplano), and a rich moss green in velvet (from V V Rouleaux).

picot braid Small loops of thread along each edge add interest to these pieces of braid (05024/09, top, and 05024/01, bottom, from Colefax & Fowler). They would work well on a number of different top fabrics as they are relatively simply in their make up. The lighter stripe through the centre creates a neat, clean look. The colours are both elegant and interesting.

cord As it follows the contours of the furniture, cord has a similar effect to single piping. However, it is often slightly larger in diameter and is made from different coloured threads, so it has a bigger impact. Flanged cord (cord attached to a cotton panel, top) can be sewn between two pieces of top fabric. This two-tone cord (31181 from Wemyss Houlès) adds sophistication, while antique gold cord (38001 from Wemyss Houlès) creates a touch of opulence, working well with many colours including black.

braid There are a great many styles of braid both in plain or combined colours. These three braids are quite individual. The first (Jute Braid AJJB1 from Altiplano) works wonderfully on a plain cream fabric background, offering a neutral and subtle finish. The second (31145 from Wemyss Houles) combines black thread and metallic gold thread extremely well on a dusty green background; together the linear black and spherical gold create an interesting and slightly unusual look. The third (Floral Braid 39093, from Wendy Cushing) is a rich combination of grape-red and gold, offering a very elegant finish.

finishes and trimmings

Trimming is used for one of two reasons: to hide a tack line or to enhance a piece. There are, however, some examples, such as the chair on page 98, where no finish is needed. Single piping, double piping, ribbon, cord, flanged cord, braid, picot braid, gimp, studs… there is a never-ending choice of trimmings with which to complete your upholstery.

The trimming is as important as the top fabric, so every effort should be made to find just the right one – it can cause the success or downfall of a piece of furniture. Deciding on the style of trimming is not always easy, and once decided, finding the right colour, texture, and design can take time, simply because there is so much choice. If you are unable to find exactly what you are looking for, there are companies who will make up a finish in your chosen colours.

Try narrowing down the style and having an idea of what colour you want before you go hunting as this will accelerate the process. Consider the top fabric: is it plain or elaborate, patterned or with a texture? Also think about the overall style and character of the chair. Using a top fabric with a strong pattern will narrow down the choice of finishings.

fan edged Both of these trimmings have a small fan edge along the bottom, one a little more elaborate than the other. The first (31092 from Wemyss Houlès) is mainly a marshy green thread highlighted with tan and yellow, the whole effect refined by the use of silver thread stitched through the centre. The second trimming (31140 also from Wemyss Houlès) is rather more plain with two colours in complementary neutral shades. Its very simplicity, relieved by the slight fan edging, makes it very effective.

suede Both of these suede trimmings (suede from Altiplano) are fairly substantial (25mm/1in) but used in conjunction with leather, on an ottoman for example, would produce a fantastic finish. They would also work well in combination with spaced antique-finish studs creating quite a striking look.

For example, the bold pattern on the fabric used for the chair on page 90 called for a plain trimming, in this case simple, brown double piping, which also emphasized the clean lines of the chair; a more colourful, elaborate trimming would have battled for attention with the top fabric. A trimming might pick out a colour that is in the top fabric or it may add another shade of the same colour. The stool on page 138 has a trimming in the same colour but in a contrasting texture, combining luxurious satin against soft, sumptuous velvet. In some cases, the trimming will lie between the top fabric and the show wood and so both should be taken into consideration when making your choice.

Ask for samples to take home with you to try on the piece and against the fabric. Before buying, carefully measure up the piece of furniture and add a little extra for good measure and turning under.

gimp There are many styles of gimp available, some adding quite an elaborate touch. Gimps in single colours or complementary shades, such as this ruby red gimp (IF 4532-417 from Turnell & Gigon), will have an understated and delicate effect, while contrasting shades, such as this gold and cream pattern on a black background (31087 from Wemyss Houles), will create a sophisticated and luxurious finish.

ribbon Velvet ribbons (10130, top, and 10131, bottom, from VV Rouleaux) are available in a variety of widths. Despite their vibrant colours, these two would add an understated and sophisticated finish to a chair. Choose ribbon made from a thickish fabric, such as velvet, for finishing so the glue used to attach them does not soak through.

studs Studs have a long history in upholstery and are very versatile. They are available in a variety of colours, sizes, and head shapes (such as domed, flat, or patterned). These studs are in antique finish, which will complement most leathers. Studs can be applied side by side or at spaced intervals, or they can be applied over another finish, such as gimp, ribbon, or braid, to give an interesting result.

other Under the right circumstances, less conventional forms of finishing add flair and detail (see page 128). Careful thought should be given to using these trimmings as they are delicate and less easily secured than traditional finishes, such as gimp or braid. The top two (Flo—019320 and Flo—10241 from VV Rouleaux) create a light effect. The third (Flo—04418 from VV Rouleaux) would be best on a decorative item, rather than a piece of furniture in daily use.

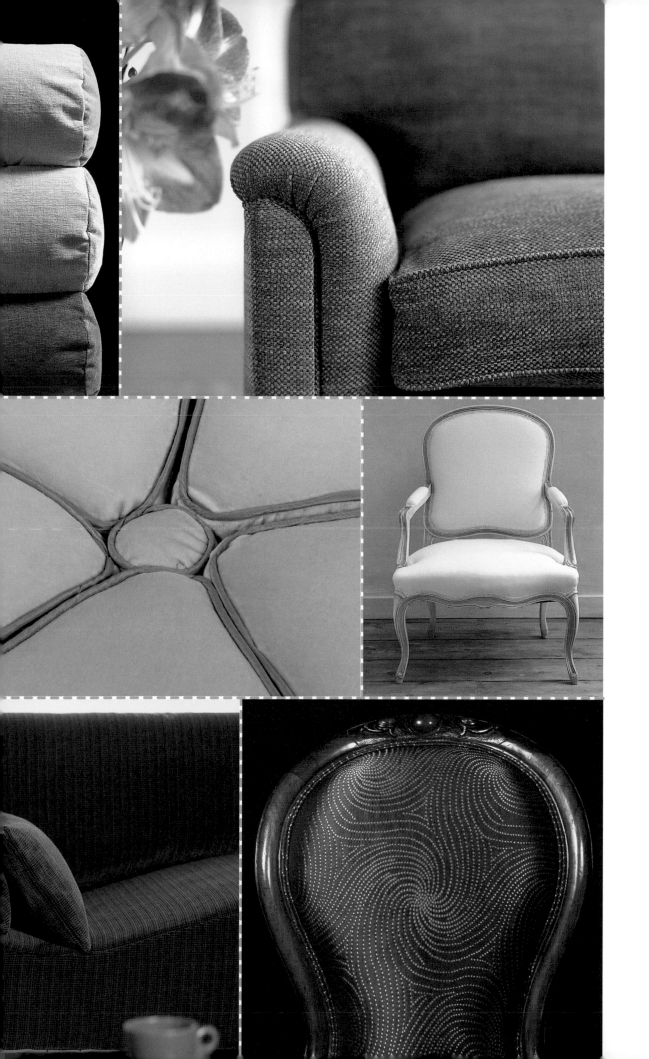

basic techniques

planning order of work

Before embarking on upholstering a piece of furniture, prepare your work space and ensure you have all the tools you may need to hand, and check that you have all the materials you may require in sufficient quantities. Doing these checks now will make the upholstering process go far more smoothly. Also take a little time to consider the piece of furniture you will be working on, appreciating its shape, character, and form, before removing the old layers and choosing the top fabric. It is often helpful to take "before" photographs of the item from each angle (front, back, and sides) to remind you of its original shape. When working on a piece of furniture, be prepared to move it around to gain access to awkward corners, and to enable you to work from the optimum angle.

Most pieces of furniture are subject to daily wear and tear and so the upholstery needs to be sturdy enough to withstand such use. As upholstery is a time-consuming process, it is well worth taking care to be accurate in all that you do. If any aspect of the work is done poorly, it may compromise the life of the item. If something is not quite coming out right, leave it and come back to it when you are in a different frame of mind. Various important stages and elements of upholstery are outlined below.

estimate materials
Sometimes the old materials, such as springs or horsehair, can be reused, however, often new materials will be required. When estimating materials needed, err on the generous side – scrimping and running out of something before you have finished is frustrating. Remember to order in advance, so you have all the materials to hand.

stripping back
Take time to fully appreciate the character and make up of the piece of furniture. Be prepared to remove each layer of material individually, as this will help you understand how it was originally put together and will help you in the rebuilding process.

restoring
After you have stripped back a piece of furniture and before you have begun any new work on it, consider the condition of the wood. Restoration can consist of a simple repolishing, which can be done at home, although it is worth taking it to a specialist restorer so the best finish is

achieved (in some cases furniture can be taken to a restorer before it is stripped back). Now is also the time to check for woodworm and take appropriate action.

order of working
With a chair or sofa, it is usually best to begin the reupholstering process with the seat, before the inside arms and inside back intrude on the space around it, making it more awkward to complete. Next, the inside arms are prepared, then the inside back, followed by the outside arms and the outside back. This is a typical sequence, however, depending on the design and make up of a piece of furniture, the order may differ. In time, you will find your own

preferred way of working. The table opposite outlines the typical sequence of work for a sprung, stuffed easy chair.

tacking
Tacks are used at various different stages in the upholstery process. Therefore, it is a good idea to get into the habit of applying them properly from the very beginning. In general, the first tack on a rail is placed in the centre, with subsequent tacks applied from the centre out to the corners of a piece of furniture. The corners are usually left tack-free to allow for cuts and folds to be made around them, after which tacks are applied to secure the fabric, calico, or hessian in place. Applying tacks at spaced

intervals will allow room for the tacks that secure subsequent layers of material and top fabric. Often temporary tacks are placed first and then hammered home once the fabric is in the right place. To place a temporary tack, hammer it in only halfway, leaving the head sitting proud. Position several tacks in this way and once the fabric is sitting correctly, drive them home by hammering them until their heads lie flush with the rail surface. The position of a temporary tack is far easier to adjust than that of a tack that has been hammered home.

tension

Achieving the correct tension in a panel of hessian, calico, or top fabric on a seat, arm, or any other part of a piece of furniture is an important part of the upholstery process. If the fabric is too loose it will wrinkle over time and if it sits too tightly it may eventually be pulled away from the tacks. Each panel of fabric should be taut but not tight. You should aim to achieve consistent tension and balance across the whole of the area that it covers.

calico

This penultimate part of the upholstery process is key – it is at this stage that the final shape of a seat, arm, or inside back is achieved. The top fabric merely rests on top of the calico, which does all the work, so it is important to take time when applying the calico. Be prepared to manipulate the stuffing and cotton felt underneath into shape and ensure that you place neat tacks and trim away any excess. If the shape of the seat or arm is not quite right, go back to the

earlier stages and correct whatever is causing the problem. Stand back once you have applied the calico and take a look at each of the shapes you have created. Make sure they are gently rounded, symmetrical, and all the edges are neat and secure.

order of work for a typical sprung, stuffed easy chair	
what needs to be done	Consider the current condition of the piece of furniture and what will need to be done to reupholster it.
estimate materials	Work out what quantities of material are needed; if the piece still has its old covering on, the top fabric can also be measured.
strip back old coverings and materials (if appropriate)	Remove each layer individually, deciding which materials might be reusable and what work needs to be done.
webbing	If working from the bare frame, attach the webbing with tacks.
springs (if appropriate)	Replace the springs or position new ones – secure and lash them down.
hessian	Tack a layer of hessian over the webbing or springs.
bridle ties	Make a series of loops to secure the stuffing.
stuffing	Add the stuffing under the bridle ties and pull them in.
hessian	Add another layer of hessian over the stuffing.
stuffing ties	Secure the stuffing with a series of stuffing ties going through to the base of the seat.
wall and roll edge	Add strength and shape to the seat edge where necessary.
stuffing	Add more stuffing to fill out any gaps created by the roll and wall stitches.
cotton felt	Add a layer of cotton felt.
calico	Attach a layer of calico to help define the shape.
top fabric	Attach the top fabric.
trimmings	Add studs, piping, or other finishes at this stage.
dust cloth	Attach a dust cloth to the underside of the piece of furniture.

stripping back

When reupholstering any item of furniture, the first task is to strip it back, removing the old top fabric and some or all of the existing stuffing and springs (you will need to take a good look at the chair to decide which parts should be discarded). The work is best done outside or in a well-ventilated room as this is a dusty and dirty job. You will need a large dust sheet, to catch the old stuffing, and a work bench, it is a good idea to gather all the tools you will be using before you start. A large bin or bin bag along with a dustpan and brush will also help you to keep things tidy as you work.

tools
Cabriole hammer, craft knife, large dust sheet, mallet, pincers, ripping chisel, scissors, staple puller, tack lifter.

step 1 Decide how much of the stuffing and springs need to be removed. In this case the whole chair needs to be stripped back. Some of the springs in the seat were out of shape, the stuffing on the seat, although still compact was rather lumpy so both of these needed to be replaced and rebuilt. The materials on the arms and wings were clearly worn out so these needed to be stripped right back too. Stripping back this chair will take time as there are a lot of studs around the frame of the chair that need to be removed carefully in order to avoid splitting or damaging the wooden frame. Take photographs of the piece before you begin work; when you begin to reupholster, they will help you to get the shape of the seat correct as well as show where the various seams were originally.

step 2 Always work from the bottom upwards. Position the chair on the workbench so it can be easily worked on and begin by removing the old tacks or staples from the dust cloth on the base of the seat. This can be discarded straight away.

step 3 Remove all the old tacks and staples from the areas you will be restoring. This leaves a good clean carcase to work on. Place the ripping chisel under the head of each tack and use the mallet to knock it out. Ensure you are working with the grain to avoid splitting the wood. Take care when removing tacks and staples from show wood (wood that will remain visible), in this case around the top of each leg. A cabriole hammer and a staple puller or pincers may be more suitable for the delicate work required around the show wood.

step 4 Take off the top fabric. Remove it carefully as it will be helpful for sizing up new fabric and to use as a template. Begin by removing the fabric from the outside chair back, followed by the outside arms, the inside back, the inside arms, and then the seat. Use a pair of scissors to cut through the seams and stitches and make the work easier. To help you to understand how the chair was put together, remove the stuffing layer by layer and note how and where the pieces were secured. Note how many springs were used, where they were placed on the old webbing, and their size. Use a craft knife to cut through the twine holding the springs to the hessian and webbing.

step 5 Decide which, if any, of the old materials can be reused. Springs should still stand up straight. Test their "springability" against a new spring; often there is quite a difference and you may decide in favour of new springs. Old horsehair is sometimes worth reusing but it's a good idea to clean it first. Do this by placing the hair in an old

pillowcase, tied tightly or sewn at the top, and either hand washing it or taking it to the laundrette (don't risk contaminating your own machine with ancient dust mites).

step 6 Check for woodworm holes. If you come across evidence of worm, strip the whole chair of any remaining coverings and treat it all. There is little point in only treating the area that you can see, as the worm may also be active within the rest of the frame. Treatments for woodworm can be found at your local DIY outlet. Afterwards, leave the chair for several days to allow the treatment to work and dry off and also for the fumes to disappear. Woodworm or not, you may decide to send your chair to a wood restorer to make sure the wood is in good condition before you spend any more time on it. A wood restorer may treat any woodworm for you and will be able to tell you whether it is still active. If there is any show wood this can be polished at the same time.

applying webbing

Webbing forms the platform upon which all the rest of the upholstery is based; it is, therefore, important to make it secure and firm with uniform spacing. Webbing on the seat of a chair is attached either to the top of the seat frame (as in this example) or, if springs are being used, to the underside of the seat rails. It is usually secured with a fold over the top rather than underneath, as this creates a stronger foundation. Where springs are used, ensure the weave is close enough to take the diameter of the spring; leave only 3–4cm (1¼–1½in) between each length. Webbing should not be positioned too near the back uprights or corners of a chair. However, this may be necessary if a seat is wider at the front than at the back (as here), and the strips will also have to be closer to each other at the back. To avoid wastage, work from a roll of webbing, not pre-cut strips.

tools
Magnetic hammer, scissors, web strainer.

materials
16mm (⅝in) tacks, 5cm (2in) webbing.

reference
Webbing a chair back: p115, webbing an arm: p115.

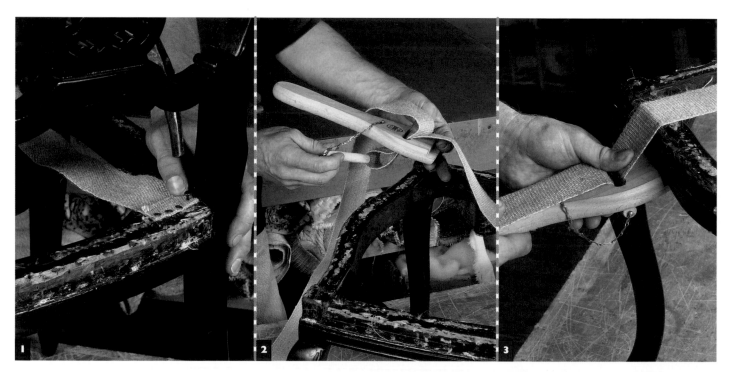

step 1 Working from the back of the chair frame to the front, secure the webbing on the top of the back rail. Make a fold of about 2.5cm (1in) in the end of the webbing. Hold the fold in place with one hand and, with the other, hammer in four tacks, working from one side of the webbing to the other and leaving a small gap between each tack.

step 2 Now take the web strainer and fold the webbing, feeding it through the horizontal slot and then placing the wooden batten through the loop you have created (the recess, or lip, at the top end of the stretcher should be facing upwards). Take hold of the loose end of the webbing and draw the loop in tight.

step 3 Using the web strainer, pull the webbing tight across the seat frame to the front of the chair. Place the stretcher so that the recessed lip at its top rests on the underneath of the chair frame (protect delicate show wood with a piece of soft cloth or leather). Lever the stretcher to create the right amount of tension on the webbing – it should feel fairly taut.

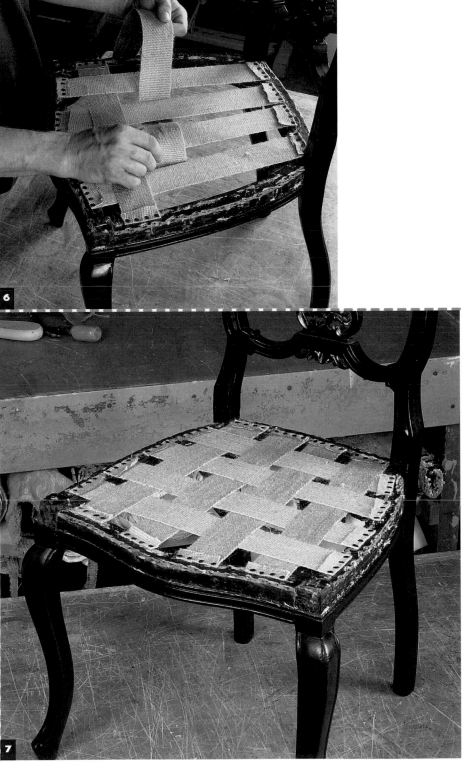

step 4 Hammer in three tacks to hold the strip in place and then cut the webbing, allowing for a fold of 2.5cm (1in).

step 5 Fold over the end of the webbing and hammer in four tacks to secure it. Take care not to hammer over the tacks underneath; you will be able to feel them under the fold. Repeat steps 1 to 5, until you have filled the seat area from front to back with evenly spaced strips of webbing.

step 6 Now attach the webbing that runs from side to side. First, weave the strip of webbing over and under the webbing that runs from the back to the front of the seat, then attach it to the frame as before. Work from the front of the frame to the back, securing the first strip just in from the seat corners.

step 7 The chair is now ready to be fitted with the base layer of hessian.

applying base hessian

Hessian is the next layer to be applied after webbing and, like the webbing, makes a strong foundation on which to build the subsequent layers of stuffing. The hessian acts as a support to ensure the stuffing remains intact, does not fall through the seat, and retains its shape, so it is important that it is good quality – 285g (10oz) hessian is ideal. If, however, a piece of furniture is sprung, the springs will lay directly on top of the webbing with the hessian to follow, helping hold the springs in place.

tools
Magnetic hammer, scissors.

materials
Hessian, 13mm (½in) tacks.

reference
Cuts, corners, and folds: pp158–9.

step 1 Measure how much hessian is required, allowing an extra 10cm (4in) all around. Cut the hessian and place it over the frame of the chair, taking care that the weave lies straight as this will help to create the right tension across the frame when it is attached.

step 2 Starting at the back, fold over the hessian before fixing it to the centre of the back frame with a tack. Hammer home the tack. Gently pull the hessian taut across to the front of the frame, keeping its weave straight, and place a temporary tack in the centre of the front rail, without folding over the hessian this time. Repeat this process on one side of the frame and then the other, again creating some tension. Once you are confident that the hessian is lying straight and the three tacks are in the right place, hammer them home.

step 3 Working out from the centre point of the back rail, fix tacks at intervals of approximately 2cm (¾in), with the hessian folded over. Leave a space of about 5cm (2in) at each corner.

step 4 Fix tacks to the front rail, working out from the centre but this time without folding over the hessian. Keep checking its position and tension as you go. Again, leave a space of 5cm (2in) at each corner. When the hessian is secure, fold it over and fix more tacks, spaced in between those underneath. Repeat this process on one of the side rails. With the last side rail, fold over the hessian before fixing the tacks.

step 5 To work around the uprights at the seat back, use scissors to make a straight cut from the corner of the hessian into the corner of the upright.

step 6 Fold the hessian down around each back upright, placing a tack on either side of it. Trim off any surplus material from around the corner. Then complete the line of tacks along the two edges of hessian leading to the upright.

step 7 Fit the hessian around the front corners: hold down one side of the folded hessian and place a tack 2cm (¾in) away from the corner; now do the same with the hessian on the other side of the corner. This will leave a lip of hessian that can be easily trimmed away; use the scissors to make a straight cut at an angle of 45 degrees to the corner.

step 8 Trim the excess hessian from around the inside of the frame, taking care to leave an edge of 1.5cm (½in) from each row of tacks.

top stuffing

Top stuffing is one of the more simple upholstery tasks to undertake and it is a process that can be completed in a relatively short amount of time. Originally, top-stuffed seats were not intended to be sat on for long periods, they were more likely to be used as occasional or decorative chairs and for this reason they contain comparatively little stuffing. As this is a relatively straight forward exercise to undertake it is a good one to start with if you are a beginner in upholstery.

tools
Circular needle, craft knife, magnetic hammer, scissors, staple gun (optional), web strainer.

materials
Calico, cotton felt, fibre, hessian, stitching twine, 13mm (½in) tacks, webbing.

reference
Bridle ties: p162, knots: p164.

step 1 Fix the webbing to the top of the frame, inside the recessed lip. For a seat frame of this size (35cm/14in by 39cm/15½in), you will need to use two webs from back to front and two from side to side. Next, attach the hessian, again working within the frame, leaving a space of about 1.5cm (½in) around the edge of the recessed lip. This will give room for the top fabric to be attached to the frame without the layers of fabric bunching up or becoming too thick.

step 2 Create a series of loops (bridle ties) to hold the stuffing in place. Do this by first securing the stitching twine to the hessian, 6cm (2½in) in from the edge, using a slip knot.

step 3 Start at the outside and work in to the centre, creating bridle ties at intervals of about 10cm (4in). (The loops can be made in a continuous ring, as shown, or they may be stitched so each one goes back on itself, see page 162). The loops should be large enough to allow your hand to go underneath. At the end, secure the twine with a locking knot.

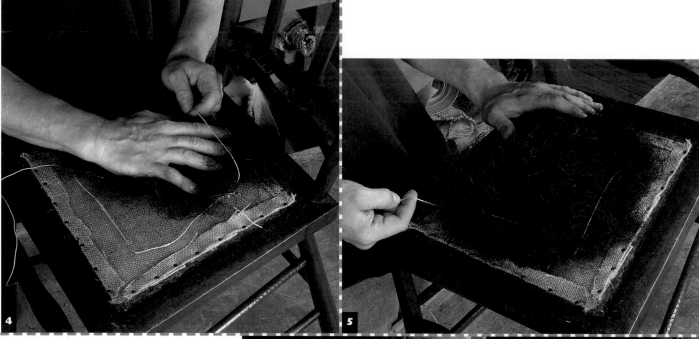

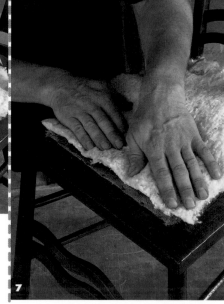

step 4 Beginning at the back of the seat and gradually working to the front, gently lift the loops and place a handful of stuffing fibre underneath them. Make sure you use plenty of fibre and tease out any lumps.

step 5 Once there is a good heap of fibre under the loops, carefully pull each loop tighter so they hold the fibre more firmly in place. Start this process where you made the first loop and work your way around each one. Tie off any excess twine at the end. Place both your hands on the finished stuffing to make sure there are no lumps, hollows, or uneven areas.

step 6 Add a layer of cotton felt. This will create a smooth layer on which to place the calico. Measure the amount needed and add a 5cm (2in) allowance all round. Place the cotton felt on top of the fibre. With one hand, press down on the felt, and with the other, gently pull away the excess from around the edges.

step 7 Check that the felt rests just within the outer edge of the hessian as the process of pulling the calico taut across the felt will bring it closer to the edges. If the cotton felt is applied right to the edges, it will get caught up when you tack down the calico.

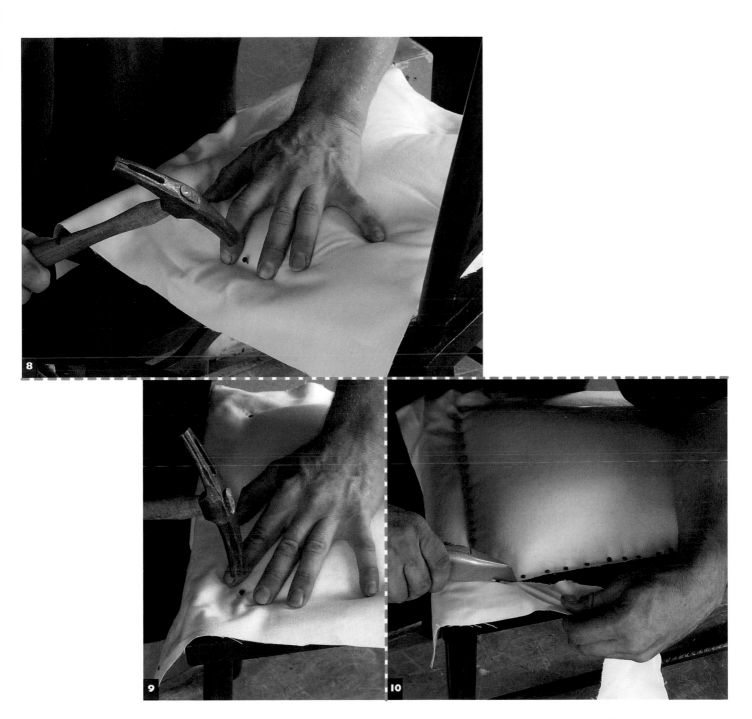

step 8 Measure and cut the calico, adding a 7cm (3in) allowance. Holding the calico in place over the cotton felt, place centre tacks first on the back lip, then the front, and then on both sides. Position the tacks just inside the rim of the lip. When placing each of these four tacks, smooth and gently pull the calico over the top of the stuffing, creating some tension and ensuring the weave is lying straight. In the example shown, the calico is not folded under; this minimizes the number of layers the top fabric will sit on.

step 9 Put four corner tacks in place, all the time maintaining the tension across the stuffing and pressing the calico out to the corners to help avoid wrinkles and lumpy ridges. Continue placing tacks, working from the centre tacks out towards the corners. Place the tacks at intervals of 1cm (½in).

step 10 Trim away the excess calico using a craft knife. Take care to cut away from you, not towards your body, and make sure you avoid touching the show wood. The seat is now ready for the top fabric.

over stuffing

An over-stuffed seat pad is used on chairs to make them more comfortable over a longer period of time. In effect, the seat is stuffed twice. Initially a layer of stuffing is positioned and held in place by a row or more of stitches, which creates a firm wall. This is followed by another series of stitches that makes a rolled edge, resulting in a stronger platform to sit on. Once this is finished, a second layer of stuffing is applied. The technique described here takes considerable time and patience, but does get easier with practice. There are several clearly defined stages, so it does not all have to be done at once. Success relies on achieving the right balance of stuffing. If you are restuffing an old chair, it may be possible to see a mark on the back uprights showing the point where the original stuffing came to, which can be a helpful guide as to how much stuffing to use. Creating a good series of wall and roll stitches will also help the end result as they give definition to the shape of the finished seat.

tools
Craft knife, double-ended needle, magnetic hammer, marker pen, regulator, scissors, staple gun (optional), web strainer, wood rule.

materials
Calico, cotton felt, stuffing fibre, hessian, stitching twine, 13mm (½in) tacks, webbing.

reference
Applying webbing: pp42–3, applying hessian: p44, cuts, corners, and folds: pp158–9, bridle ties: p162, wall and roll stitching: pp160–1.

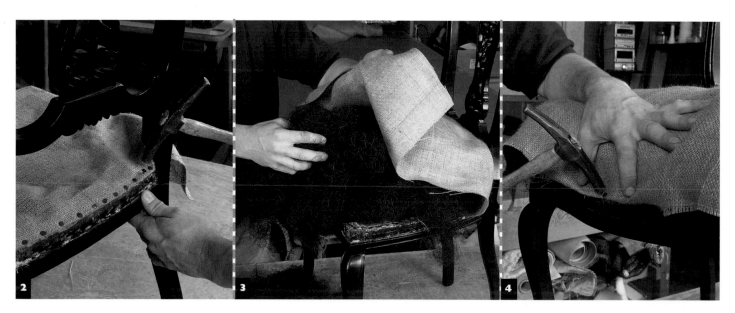

step 1 Create a platform of webbing attached to the top side of the frame, with four webs from back to front and four from side to side. Attach a layer of hessian and then make a series of bridle ties with which to hold the stuffing.

step 2 Cut sufficient hessian to cover the seat area with a 20cm (8in) allowance all around. Fold under a 2.5cm (1in) hem on one side of the hessian and tack this to the back rail, working from the centre out to the sides. This second layer of hessian will hold the stuffing in place.

step 3 Ease the fibre between the two layers of hessian. For a walled and rolled edge on a seat, you need a large quantity of stuffing to give fullness and strength. Tease out any knots along the way and pay particular attention to the edges of the seat where the stuffing will need to be quite firm.

step 4 When you are confident you have added enough stuffing, attach the front and side edges of the hessian, again folding it under. Begin by placing three tacks to the centre of the front rail and then three tacks to each of the side rails. As you pull the hessian taut over the stuffing, continually

check that the weave remains straight. Initially applying temporary tacks will help with this process. Take care that no stuffing gets caught along the tack line. Next, place the remaining tacks, working from the centre tacks out to the corners and leaving a 5cm (2in) space at each corner. Create a fold around each of the front corners of the seat, securing it with two tacks. Make a straight cut into the hessian at each back upright, fold the excess material under, and secure it with a tack. (For more details on making cuts and folds around corners, see pages 158–9.)

step 5 Use a regulator to tease the stuffing into the desired position along the edges of the seat, ensuring there are no lumps. Gently manipulate the fibre around, working little by little, rather than trying to move big chunks. The end result should feel compact and even.

step 6 The chair is now ready for a row of wall stitches, which effectively pulls the stuffing to the side of the frame to create a firm edge. Indicate where the stitches will go by using a marker pen and ruler to draw a straight line just above the tacks and approximately 8cm (3in) away from the top edge of the seat on all four sides. On the seat shown here, only one row of wall stitch is needed. With deeper padding, more would be required, at intervals of 2.5cm (1in).

step 7 Thread plenty of stitching twine on the double-ended needle and insert it at the back right-hand side of the chair, on the line you have marked. Push the needle up at an angle aiming to bring it out 5cm (2in) away from the front edge and pull it through until you can just see the twine. Do not pull the threaded end out of the stuffing, instead push it back in to the seat, angled so that it appears 2cm (¾in) along from where it was originally inserted. Take the needle out and make a slip knot with the two lengths of twine. Insert the needle again 4cm (1½in) along from the slip knot, angle it and pull it through as before until you can just see the twine coming out of the hessian. Again, without pulling the threaded end out, push

the needle back in to the seat again so that it comes out at the end of the last stitch. Bring the needle only half way out and loop one end of the twine around the needle three times and then pull the needle out completely taking it through the loops. Lock the knot by pulling it first to the right and then the left until it tightens, feeling the fibre being pulled closer to the edge of the seat. Continue stitching in this way along the first side, the front, and the remaining side, tying the twine off at the end with a locking knot. Secure a new length of twine to stitch along the back of the chair.

step 8 Mark up the chair for the roll stitch. Draw a second line 2.5cm (1in) above the first one on all sides of the seat. Then mark another line around the top of the seat approximately 5cm (2in) in from the edge. Work the regulator on the top of the seat, eliminating knots and gently encouraging the stuffing to the edge so a roll can be created.

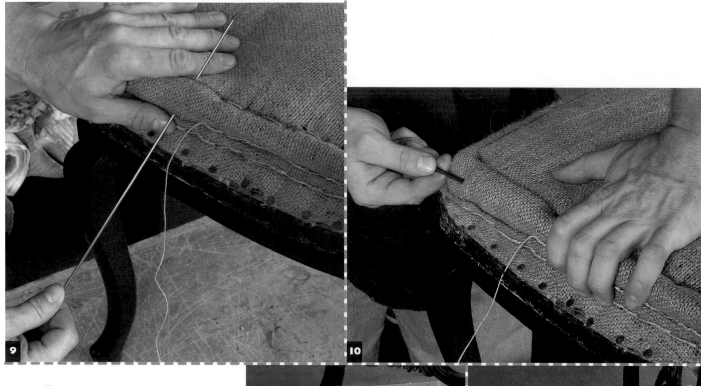

step 9 Thread a long length of twine on to the double-ended needle. Beginning on the right-hand side of the seat near the back upright, insert the needle on the line marked in the side and up through the line marked on top. Pull it out at the top and then reinsert it 2.5cm (1in) further along, making a visible stitch, pushing the threaded end out the side again and making a slip knot in the loose end. Reinsert the needle, bring it out on top as before, then reinsert it 2.5cm (1in) further along, bringing it out at the side again. Make a knot by wrapping the thread around the needle three times.

step 10 Repeat step 9 to complete the roll edge stitch along all the sides, front, and back of the seat. As you go round, keep regulating the top edge to pull the stuffing forward as you work.

step 11 Make the stuffing in the centre of the seat firmer with a series of stuffing ties. To do this, thread the needle with a length of stitching twine and secure it with a slip knot at the back corner. Pushing the needle right through the pad and webbing, work your way towards the centre of the seat. The stitches on the top of the seat should be about 7cm (3in) long and the same apart.

step 12 Apply another layer of stuffing to the centre of the seat as the stuffing stitches will have compressed it, creating a small concave area in the middle of the seat. Only a small amount of stuffing is needed on this occasion, just enough to fill out any spaces.

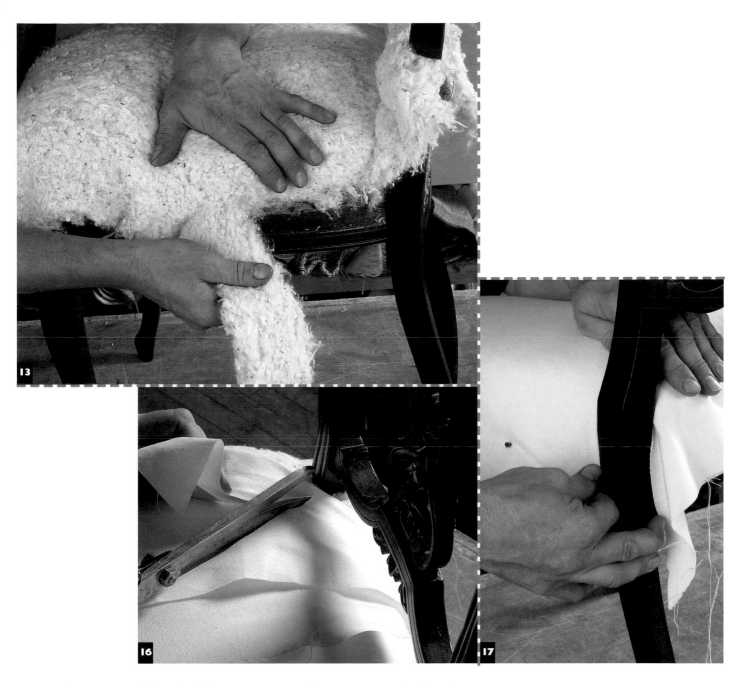

step 13 Create a smooth layer by adding enough cotton felt on top of the fibre to cover the seat easily. Place one hand on the felt and use the other hand to gently pull it down along the sides of the seat to about 2.5cm (1in) above the tack line. When the calico is applied, it will pull the cotton felt down further. By leaving this space, you avoid any lumps of felt getting caught in it.

step 14 Cut the calico for the seat with an additional allowance of 10cm (4in). Place it over the cotton felt and temporarily place one centre tack on each side, gently pulling the calico across to create the right tension.

step 15 Place temporary tacks along the seat rails from the centre tacks to the corners of the chair. Work the calico as you go, ensuring the weave lies straight and checking you are creating a good overall shape. The calico creates the finished shape of the seat so the top fabric can be attached without being "worked".

step 16 Cut a straight line into the corner of each back upright, leaving approximately 1.5cm (½in) from the upright uncut.

step 17 Pull the calico down each side of the upright, folding it under and smoothing it into position. Secure the calico either side of the upright with a tack, trimming away any excess. Repeat the process on the other back corner.

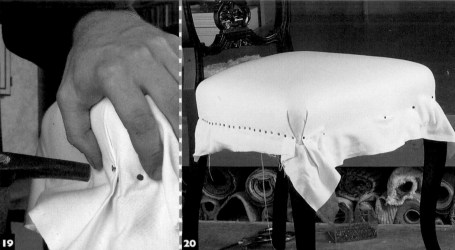

step 18 Smooth the calico flat over the front corner and hold it in place with a tack on either side.

step 19 Take the excess calico from one side, pull it across to make a neat fold and apply a tack to hold it in place. Repeat this on the other side of the corner. Repeat the same process on the remaining front corner.

step 20 Tack the rest of the calico into place. Work on one side of the seat, from the centre out to the corners, then the other side. Then complete the back, followed by the front. It is very important to continually smooth the calico into shape, creating firm contours and making sure there are no lumps on top or along the sides and no cotton felt caught up along the tack line. Placing temporary tacks greatly helps this process as these tacks can easily be taken out while the calico is manipulated into place and then replaced.

step 21 Once all the tacks are in place and you have created a perfect shape, trim away the excess calico with a craft knife. The chair is now ready for the top fabric.

springing

Springs are used in upholstered furniture to give additional comfort, strength, and stability, and to help seats, arms, and chair backs to keep their shape over time. Different types and sizes of springs are used for the various parts of a piece of furniture and also differ depending on the size of the piece. As a rule, nine-gauge springs are good seating quality, giving a firm but not rigid seat. The springs are secured to the webbing, to each other, and then to the frame of the piece of furniture. They are also secured to a layer of hessian that is positioned over the top of them. It is very important that they are attached securely so that they keep their form and work together as a unit. In this example, the springs on a nineteenth century chair are replaced.

tools
Craft knife, magnetic hammer, scissors, spring needle, staple gun (optional), tailor's chalk, web strainer.

materials
Hessian, laid cord, springs, stitching twine, 13mm (½in) tacks, 16mm (⅝in) tacks, webbing.

reference
Stripping back: pp40–41, applying webbing: pp42–3, cuts, corners, and folds: pp158–9, stitches: pp160–3, knots: p164.

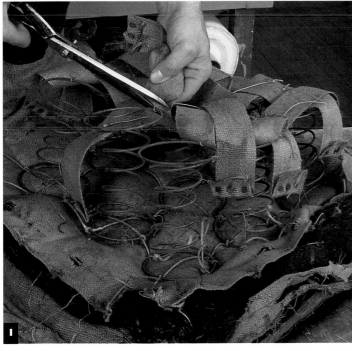

step 1 Strip back the chair, cutting the old springs away from the base. Check to see if they can be reused. Springs can be used again as long as they are still standing absolutely straight and compress well. To test an old spring, press down on it with the palm of your hand, if it compresses down in a line, it is fine, but if it bends out to the side, it should be replaced. It is not advisable to combine new and old springs so if one spring needs to be renewed, replace them all. Keep the old top covering of hessian to remind you how many springs were originally used and their arrangement.

step 2 Attach new webbing to the underside of the seat frame, creating a base on which to place the springs. On this chair there are four webs from front to back and five from side to side. Space the webbing strips close enough so that the springs cannot slip down between the gaps.

step 3 Begin the springing process by placing the springs on top of the webbing, leaving a gap of approximately 3cm (1¼in) between their bases. Leave a space of 5cm (2in) around the side rails and 10cm (4in) around the back rails to allow for the fullness of the inside back padding. Place the springs no more than 2cm (¾in) away from the front rail as this is where the seat will get the most wear. Ensure the springs are evenly spaced so that they work as one unit. Use tailor's chalk to mark their positions on the webbing.

step 4 Attach the springs to the webbing using a spring (curved) needle to make three equidistant stitches over each spring, together forming a V-shape of twine on the underside of the webbing. Secure the twine with a slip knot at the back left-hand corner of the frame on the underside of the webbing. Push the needle up through the webbing near the first spring, then bring it back through the webbing to create a loop over the base coil of the spring. Tie this off with a single locking knot but do not cut the twine. Stitch across to the other side of the spring, and repeat the process – push the needle up through the webbing, over the base coil of the spring, and back through the webbing, tying it off with a single locking knot. Now make the third stitch in the same way, making the locking knot and then moving on to the next spring, without cutting the twine.

step 5 Continue the process until each spring has been secured by three loops, working across the back row, back along the middle row, and then across the front row. Viewed from the underneath, the twine creates an irregular pattern of connected V-shapes on the webbing. Do not cut the twine until every spring is held in place. Secure the last spring underneath with a double locking knot.

step 6 The springs are now ready to be lashed down, which is done using laid cord and a series of hitch knots. Measure enough laid cord to reach from the back of the seat frame to the front and plenty more for creating the knots. Attach the cord to the back of the frame, just behind the centre of the middle spring, by placing a 16mm (⅝in) tack on the top of the back rail, tying the cord to it with a single knot, and tapping it in lightly. Position tacks in the same way opposite the remaining springs on the back rail (here there are two), repeating the process on the front and side rails, opposite the centre of each spring. Hammer home the first tack.

step 7 Begin to lash down the springs, starting with the centre back spring. Pressing down on the spring, use a hitch knot to tie the cord to the coil third from the top. Release the pressure, take the cord to the front of the same spring and tie it to the coil second from the top, again with a hitch knot. Holding down the next spring, tie the cord to the coil second from the top at the back of the spring, take it to the front of the spring and tie it off again on the second coil. Continue to the next spring, but as this is the front spring, tie off the second hitch knot on the third coil down, not the second. Gently apply a little pressure to the front spring before tying the second knot, then tie the cord off with a simple knot around the front tack (placed earlier) and hammer it home. Cut the cord and secure the end with a second tack.

step 8 Repeat the lashing process on the two remaining rows of springs, again working from the back to the front.

step 9 Lash the springs to the side rails in the same way. As you tie them off, apply a little pressure to the back and front row of springs, as well as to the springs closest to the side rails. The centre springs should have some tension but their coils should be flat. It is important that you keep the laid cord taut throughout the whole process.

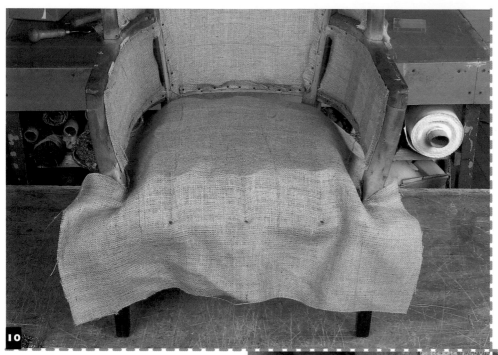

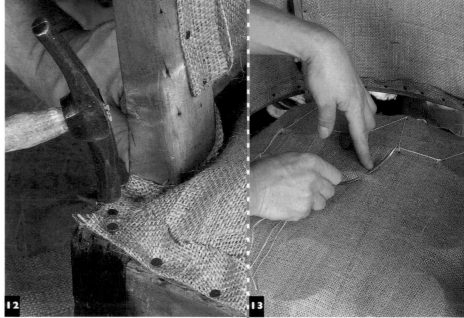

step 10 Cut a piece of hessian big enough to cover the seat frame with a 20cm (8in) allowance all round. Turn under 2cm (¾in) as a hem and then attach it to the back rail with a centre tack. Place a row of tacks from this central one out to the back uprights, stopping 5cm (2in) from the corners. Next, attach the hessian to the front rail with three evenly spaced tacks (do not make a hem yet). As you go, gently pull the hessian across the springs, ensuring the weave lies straight, to create a taut, neat fit.

step 11 Peel the hessian away from each back corner towards the centre of the seat and make a T cut towards the corner of the upright, stopping 2cm (¾in) away. Fold the hessian under around each side of the upright, and secure with a tack on either side. Do the same on the other back upright. Gently pull back the hessian back from each front arm upright from the sides in towards the centre of the chair and make a Y cut in front of each upright. Fold the hessian under around each upright and secure with a tack on each side.

step 12 Add more tacks on the front rail, working from the centre out and stopping 5cm (2in) from the corners. Repeat along the side rails. Space all the tacks widely enough to allow another series of tacks in between them. Turn over a 2cm (¾in) hem in the hessian, trimming away any excess, and secure it to the front and side rails; put the tacks between those that are already in place. As you are turning the hessian over and creating a hem, make a neat fold in each front corner above the chair legs and secure it with two tacks.

step 13 Stitch the springs to the hessian in the same way that you attached them to the webbing (step 4). Begin with a slip knot in the back right-hand corner and, using a spring needle, stitch each top coil to the hessian at three equidistant points. Begin with the back row, working from right to left, followed by the middle row, working from left to right, and then the front row, right to left again. The chair is now ready for the stuffing to be applied.

stuffing, with springs

Once springs have been secured to a chair frame, two layers of stuffing are applied, softening the impact of the springs and helping to define the shape of the seat. This is straightforward but quite time-consuming as typically a walled edge is created along the front of the seat, followed by a rolled edge above this, thereby making a secure and firm edge to the seat. To achieve the desired results be sure to have plenty of fibre to hand.

tools
Craft knife, 40cm (16in) double-ended needle, magnetic hammer, regulator, scissors.

materials
Calico, cotton felt, fibre, hessian, stitching twine, 13mm (½in) tacks.

reference
Cuts, corners, and folds: pp158–9, stitches: pp160–3 (bridle ties: p162).

step 1 To secure the stuffing, begin by creating a series of bridle ties over the layer of hessian covering the springs. Work from one corner, around the seat, and into the centre, taking care not to stitch through the springs. Next, attach a layer of hessian to the chair frame; this will hold the stuffing in place. Measure and cut sufficient hessian, including a 20cm (8in) allowance all round.

step 2 Attach the hessian to the back rail with spaced tacks, turning it under by 2cm (¾in). Then fold the hessian to the back of the seat to make room for the stuffing. Use plenty of fibre so that the springs will not be felt through the stuffing and so that you can create a firm walled and rolled edge. Place it all around the seat, behind the springs at the back, and down the outsides of the springs at the sides. Also make sure the front springs are well covered as this is where strength is needed in the seat pad. Tease out the fibres to ensure there are no lumps.

step 3 Arrange the hessian over the top of the stuffing and secure it along the top of the front rail with spaced tacks. Fit it around the uprights and arm rails, making T cuts around the back uprights and Y cuts around the front uprights, before pulling it under the arm rails and around the uprights. Create the right amount of tension over the stuffing, keeping the weave of the hessian straight. When securing the hessian, turn it under with a 2cm (¾in) hem along the top of each rail; the exception to this is when you have a selvedge, which will not fray.

step 4 Make at least one row of wall stitching and then one of roll stitching to create a firm seat edge. This seat pad is quite generous so needs three layers of wall stitching. Use a regulator during the stitching process to tease the fibres from the centre to the front and to help mould a firm edge. Further secure the stuffing using a double-ended needle to make a series of through stitches in the centre of the pad, leaving 10cm (4in) around the edges. Do this by securing the twine with a knot at a corner on the seat top and working your way into the centre, inserting the needle right through the seat. Turn the chair upside down to see where the needle is coming through. Reinsert the needle approximately 7cm (3in) away and repeat the process. Take care to avoid the springs (otherwise the twine may catch).

step 5 Add another layer of stuffing, simply laying it on top of the hessian, to fill out any holes in the centre.

step 6 Put a layer of cotton felt over the seat to create a smooth shape. Lay it over the fibre and use your hand to tuck it down the side and backs of the chair. Make sure at least 2.5cm (1in) goes down each side. Feather it to sit just above the tack line at the front of the seat; do this by placing one hand on the cotton felt and gently pulling away the excess with the other.

step 7 Cut sufficient calico to cover the seat and allow a further 15cm (6in) all round. Position it over the seat. Make T cuts around each back upright and Y cuts around each front arm upright, and pull the calico down under the arm rails and the inside back rail. Attach it to the back rail with three spaced tacks.

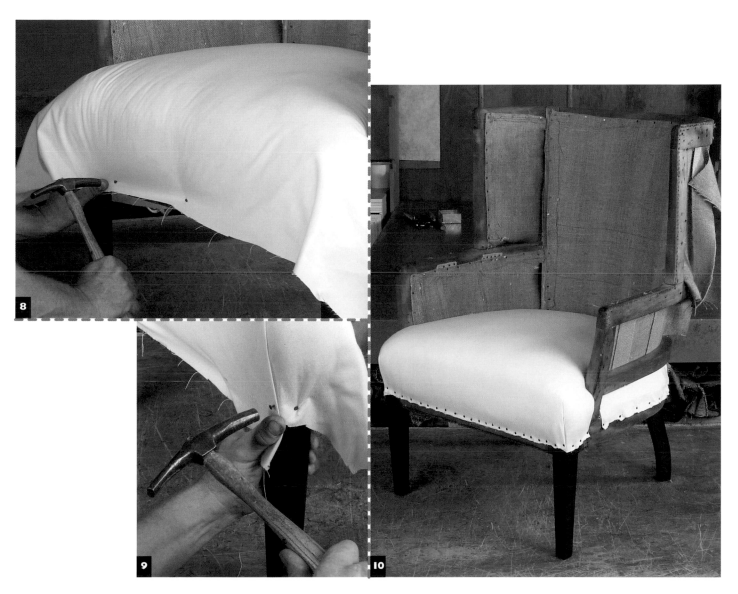

step 8 Smooth the calico over the stuffing on the seat. Be sure to create the right tension across the seat pad and keep the weave of the calico straight. Secure the calico to the front seat rail with three spaced tacks. When you work the calico around the frame, remember that you are creating the final shape of the seat upon which the top fabric will lie, so take your time.

step 9 Fold the calico around each side of the front arm uprights and secure with tacks. Continue to place tacks to the side rails and back rail. Make neat folds in the calico around each corner above the legs, pull the calico from the side around the corner to the front and secure with a tack. Trim away any excess and then make a vertical fold in the calico on the corner and secure with a tack.

step 10 Complete the tacking process, placing evenly spaced tacks along the front rail. When the calico is secure, trim it back to just below the tacking line with a craft knife. The chair is now ready for the top fabric.

deep buttoning

Deep buttoning is a time-consuming process, but patience and accuracy will contribute greatly to the end results. The buttoning technique up to calico stage is covered here (see pages 98–103 for deep buttoning on top fabric). This petite and elegant button-back chair was charming, even in its rather dilapidated state; nineteenth century button-back chairs were often made with a wooden base and a metal back frame, but this one has a wooden back with a subtle walled edge and a small rolled top. The seat pad was in good condition and so it was re-covered with only a new layer of cotton felt and calico; the stuffing on the chair back, however, was rather out of shape and needed to be completely rebuilt. This chair has a relatively small area of buttons, so such a piece is ideal for a first attempt at deep buttoning.

tools
Circular needle, double-ended needle, magnetic hammer, marker pen, scissors, tape measure, web strainer, wood rule.

materials
Calico, cotton felt, fibre, hessian, stitching twine, 13mm (½in) tacks, webbing.

reference
Applying webbing and hessian: pp42–4, over stuffing: pp48–52, cuts, corners, and folds: pp158–9 (pleating: p158), stitches: pp160–3 (bridle ties: p162), knots: p164.

step 1 Strip back the top frame of the chair to the carcase, keeping the old padding for guidance as it shows the positioning of the buttons. Attach three webs from the bottom rail to the top rail, placing one in the centre and the other two evenly spaced on each side of it. The sides of this chair back curve inwards, so it is inappropriate to web from side to side because this would prevent the stuffing from following the original curve. The curve also makes it awkward to use a web strainer; an alternative approach is to use your hand to apply firm pressure to the webbing as you pull it across the top rail and this will give it the necessary tension.

step 2 Cut sufficient hessian to cover the chair back with an allowance of 10cm (4in) all round. Attach it on the top rail with spaced tacks. Now place a centre tack on each side rail and on the bottom rail. Manipulating the hessian and ensuring the weave lies straight, gradually place evenly spaced tacks to the side and bottom rails, working from the centre to the corners. Trim away the excess hessian leaving enough to make a 2.5cm (1in) hem. Fold this over and add a further row of tacks in between those underneath. Make neat folds around each corner, trimming away the excess hessian.

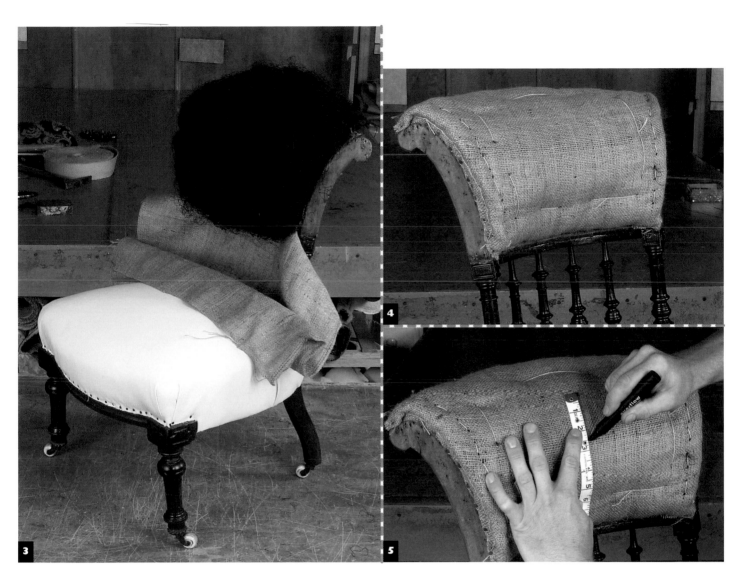

step 3 This chair back has a walled and rolled edge so needs plenty of stuffing over the hessian. Make a series of bridle ties in the hessian and gently add a good quantity of stuffing, pulling the ties in to secure it. Now attach another layer of hessian, cut with a 10cm (4in) allowance all round. Fix the hessian to the bottom rail with spaced tacks, this time turning it under rather than over. Next apply centre tacks to the top rail and side rails, each time turning the hessian under with a 2.5cm (1in) hem. Finally, place the rest of the tacks, working from the centre outwards on each rail. To achieve a good result in deep buttoning, it is important to get the fibre firmly packed in place so, if necessary, add more stuffing as you tack down the hessian.

step 4 Build the walled edge and then stitch a rolled edge (see pages 160–1). Then secure the stuffing in place with a series of through stitches around the edge of the centre of the pad. Take care not to place any of the stitches in the main part of the pad as they may interfere with the button positions.

step 5 Begin to mark up the button positions on the hessian. The old padding will be a helpful guide to how many buttons you are going to need, but if this is not available, work it out with reference to the size and shape of the chair back. In this case there will be three horizontal rows of buttons, with four buttons on the top and bottom rows and three buttons in the centre one. Use the tape measure to find the centre points along the top and the bottom. Now place the tape measure vertically between these two points to find the centre of the pad; mark this clearly. Use the tape measure in the same way on the left and right sides to find the centre points.

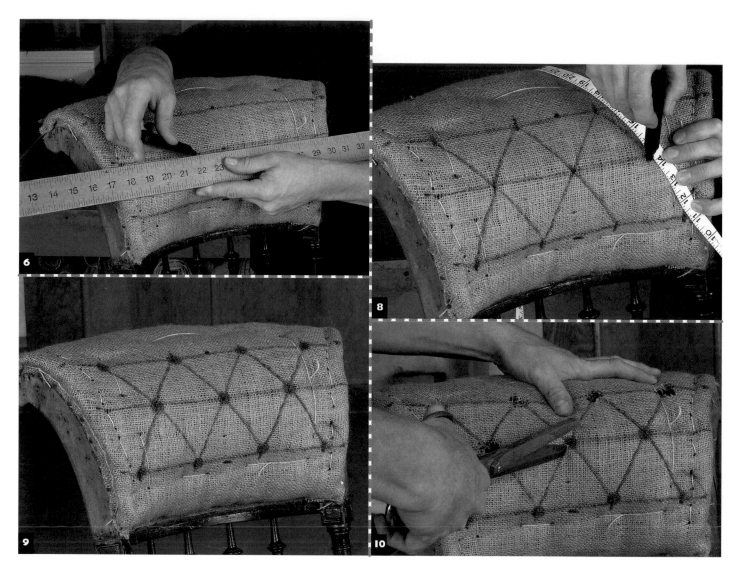

step 6 Decide on the space between each row of buttons and then, using a ruler, draw three horizontal lines running left to right across each central marking. The spacing of the rows will depend on the size, shape, and style of the chair, referring to the old top fabric at this stage is often extremely helpful. The rows on this chair are 7cm (3in) apart. Pay particular attention to the bottom row: if the inside back meets with the chair seat, ensure that the buttons begin at least 20cm (8in) above the seat.

step 7 Decide on the button spacings. The old pad of this chair indicates the buttons were at 10cm (4in) intervals. Beginning with the centre row, mark the centre point as a button then measure 10cm (4in) to each side of it and mark these button positions.

step 8 On the top line, measure 5cm (2in) out from the centre point on either side and mark two button positions. Then measure 10cm (4in) from each of these markings and indicate the remaining two button positions. Repeat these markings on the bottom row. Connect these points with diagonal lines to create diamond shapes. Typically, these diamonds are longer from top to bottom than they are from side to side. Here, they are 15cm (6in) long by 10cm (4in) wide.

step 9 Clearly mark the precise position of each button.

step 10 Make a small cut, about 1cm (½in) long, in each button marking. Push the ends of the scissors in and cut the surface of the hessian only (not into the stuffing). Push your finger through the hole and into the stuffing, easing it through the fibres until you can feel the hessian at the back of the pad.

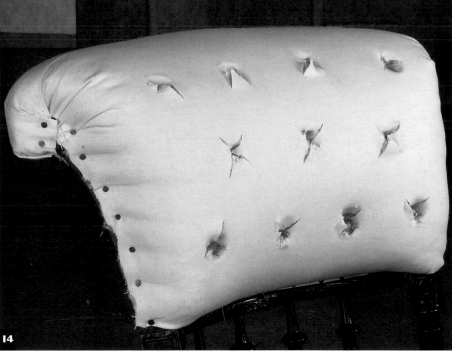

step 11 Position a layer of cotton felt. Make sure the piece is big enough to reach to the bottom of the padding and around the rolled top. Locate the button holes through the cotton felt by gently applying pressure with your hands. Having found a hole, push your finger carefully through the cotton felt.

step 12 In each case, pinch out a small amount of the cotton felt to reveal the holes underneath.

step 13 Cut a piece of calico with a 5cm (2in) allowance all round. Position it on the chair frame and turning it under on the top and bottom rails only, place four centre tacks. Gradually work around the frame applying tacks from the centre out, working the calico to ensure a firm and even fit. With a rolled top, as seen here, carefully fold and pleat the calico on the sides around the top. Trim off any excess calico from the side rails.

step 14 Using the palm of your hand, find the holes underneath the calico and make a cut in the fabric to reveal them. The chair is now ready for the top fabric.

estimating top fabric

The best way to estimate how much fabric you will need to upholster a piece of furniture is either at the calico stage (see page 39) or when the old top fabric is still intact, as this will take into account the full dimensions of the item with the stuffing in place. It is very important to get this stage right as there is nothing more frustrating than finding out you do not have sufficient fabric to complete the job. Always err on the generous side when buying fabric. It is helpful to make a rough sketch of the chair you are reupholstering and to record the measurements beside each chair part; if the fabric you want to use has a weave or pattern on it, use arrows to indicate the direction in which it will lie on the chair.

tools
Graph paper, notebook, pen, scissors, tape measure.

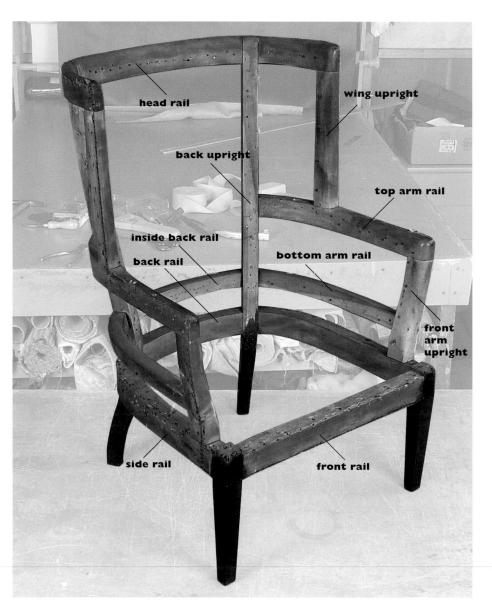

head rail

wing upright

back upright

top arm rail

inside back rail

bottom arm rail

back rail

front
arm
upright

side rail

front rail

When measuring a piece of furniture for top fabric take the tape measure to the furthest point of each section of the chair. For example the inside back should be measured from the back of the head rail, over the top of the chair and down the length of the inside back to the inside back rail. The measurements should be taken across the widest points of each part of the chair and down and around the corresponding rails of the frame. Remember to add an allowance of at least 10cm (4in) to each panel of fabric to facilitate handling.

Understanding how the frame of a chair is constructed and the names of the various parts will help you during the upholstering process. The diagram on the left shows the main components of a wing chair, while the diagram on the right shows the various measurements you will need to take to find out how much fabric you require.

outside back

outside back

outside wing

inside wing

inside back

inside arm

outside arm

seat

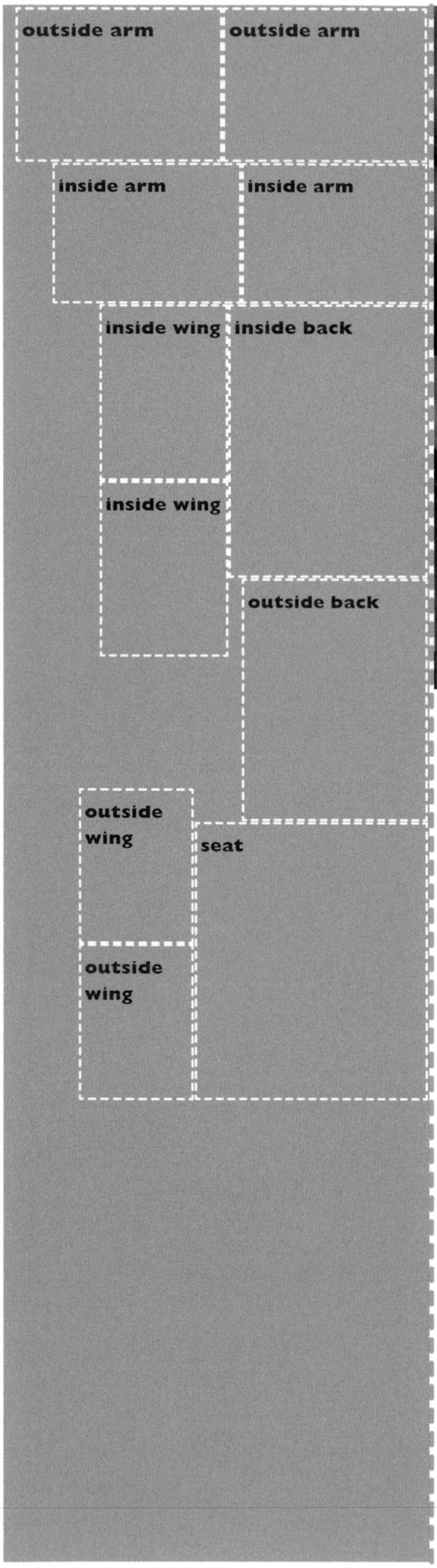

step 1 Begin by measuring the inside arm. Place the tape measure on the underside of the arm (here under the scroll) and take it around and then down between the seat and the arm to the side rail, remembering to add 10cm (4in) to each end for handling.

step 2 Measure the seat, taking the tape measure from the back rail between the back of the seat and chair back, across the seat, and over the front of the seat to the underside of the front rail. Again add 10cm (4in) to each end for handling.

step 3 Using the diagram on page 65, continue to take measurements until every part of the chair has been measured. If you are going to make piping from the fabric, adjust the amount you need accordingly or estimate whether there will be sufficient in the offcuts. Bear in mind that fabric for piping is best cut on the bias. Each piece of furniture is a little different, some chairs have front arm scrolls, others have wings and some have buttons: be sure to account for all the parts that need covering. If the piece of furniture has buttons, you will need to take the buttonholes into account when you measure for the fabric – push the tape into each hole as you measure.

step 4 Record the measurements in a table such as the one on the right. This will act as a helpful reference.

step 5 Use the measurements to draw up each chair part to scale on the graph paper. Draw up the panels to their greatest width and length and do not make them a perfect shape as the fabric will be cut to shape once it is attached to the chair. Cut out the panels and place them on a drawing of a length of fabric, scaled down to the same scale as the panels and made to the correct fabric width, also in scale (there are various standard widths, such as 127cm (50in), 140cm (55in), and 150cm (59in)). Place each of the pieces on this drawing, optimizing their positions to use the least amount of fabric possible.

plain fabric The diagram on the left is an example of how you might lay out pieces on a fabric that has no weave or pattern (this is one of several ways of laying out the fabric panels).

If you are using a fabric that has a weave or pile, such as velvet, take this into account in your calculations as the weave or pile will need to be placed on the chair in the right direction, that is from top to bottom and from the back towards the front.

chair measurements for sample chair				
	length cm (in)		width cm (in)	
inside back	88cm	(35in)	65cm	(26in)
outside back	82cm	(32in)	63cm	(25in)
seat	93cm	(37in)	79cm	(31in)
inside arm x 2	64cm	(25in)	48cm	(19in)
	64cm	(25in)	48cm	(19in)
outside arm x 2	66cm	(26in)	49cm	(19in)
	66cm	(26in)	49cm	(19in)
inside wing x 2	58cm	(23in)	42cm	(17in)
	58cm	(23in)	42cm	(17in)
outside wing x 2	53cm	(21in)	39cm	(15in)
	53cm	(21in)	39cm	(15in)

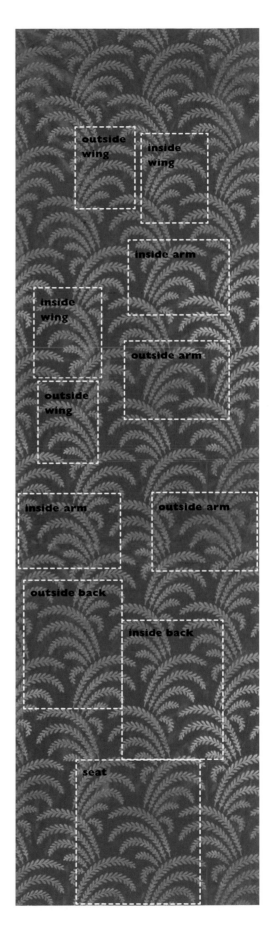

patterned fabric More fabric is needed if you are using a patterned cloth as you need to allow for the pattern repeats. Measuring up for a patterned fabric takes more time and careful consideration and planning. Measure the chair parts and create a template as before. On the fabric template, mark up where the pattern repeat occurs. The style and size of the pattern, along with the repeat, will dictate how you lay out the fabric pieces. If the fabric has a large pattern on it as with the example here (right), arrange the panels so the pattern lies in the centre. This ensures that the seat will show the main body of the pattern, as will the inside back and outside back; where possible each of the arm and wing panels should also show the main body of the pattern. In this example, each of the wing panels mirror each other with one pattern going to the right and the other to the left, creating a balance; the arm panels do the same.

If your fabric has a small often-repeated pattern, it is better to align each of the panels so the pattern follows on exactly to the adjoining panel. For example, the inside back continues the pattern from the seat. For each piece, remember to allow for the fabric that will be used to secure it to the frame, too. Once the furniture is upholstered, there should be no visual break in the pattern, with each panel matching up with the pattern on the panel next to it.

When laying out the templates on small-patterned fabric, it is easier if you place them in a certain order. Place the template for the seat first, followed by the template for the inside back, lining it up with the pattern on the seat. Next, place the parts

for the inside arms bearing in mind these should be symmetrical with each other. The outside arms should also be symmetrical, cut as a pair. Now place the outside back, making sure this matches up with the pattern for the inside back and the outside arms. From this you can work out how much fabric is needed – as you can see here, a substantially longer piece of patterned fabric is needed in comparison with the plain fabric on the opposite page.

applying top fabric

Applying the top fabric to a piece of furniture is one of the most rewarding
stages of upholstery as you finally start to see how the finished item will
look – your chair or sofa will gradually take on a different appearance as
you re-cover it in its new "top coat". The shape and outline of the piece of
furniture will have been achieved at the calico stage so there is no
moulding or shaping to be done when fitting the top fabric, however, it is
important to take time over attaching it as you will want it to be absolutely
secure and straight. When cutting out the top fabric it is usually
recommended to add a minimum of 10cm (4in) all round to help with
positioning and manipulating the fabric. (For guidance on choosing a
suitable top fabric, see pages 22–33; for estimating the amount you will
need, see pages 64–7.)

tools
Craft knife, circular needle, hammer,
scissors, sewing machine, skewers, staple
gun, tailor's chalk, upholstery pins.

materials
Back tacking strips, dust cloth, slipping
thread, 13mm (½in) tacks, top fabric.

reference
tacking: pp38–9, estimating top fabric:
pp64–7, applying a dust cloth: p83,
pleating: pp97 & 158, cuts, corners, &
folds: pp164–7, stitches: pp160–63

step 1 Lay out the fabric on your work
surface, good side down, and begin marking
up the different lengths of fabric with tailor's
chalk (use the measurements you recorded
when estimating the fabric required, pages
64–7). Draw up panels rather than actual
shapes as plenty of fabric will be needed for
handling and fitting. Take into account any
weave or pile, ensuring that it runs in the
right direction when in place on the piece of
furniture – if you put the fabric right side up
in place on the item it should feel smooth
when you run your hand from the back to
the front, or from the top to the bottom.
Also, of course, cut to allow for patterns
(see page 67). Label each piece and add
arrows to indicate top and bottom or
left- and right-hand sides.

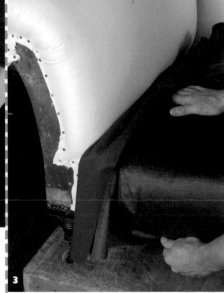

step 2 Smooth the fabric out so there are
no wrinkles and cut out each piece, cutting
away from your body.

In some cases, the width of a part of the
furniture is greater than the width of the
fabric; an additional piece of top fabric must
therefore be machine-sewn on to the
relevant panel, thereby extending it. The seat
of this sofa is wider than the fabric and two
additional pieces have been added. They are
very discreet and will be mostly hidden by
cushions. Top fabric can also be extended
below the rails using lining fabric or a
leftover piece of fabric, so avoiding any
wastage; the top fabric is not seen in these
positions anyway.

step 3 Typically, attaching the top fabric
follows this order: seat, inside arms, inside
back, outside arms, and back. Lay the fabric
good side up on the seat, smoothing it out
and making sure the panel centre sits at the
seat centre. With a pattern, take extra care
with the positioning; with a weave or pile,
again ensure this feels smooth when you run
your hand from the seat back to the front.
If you are sure the fabric is in the right
position, place spaced temporary tacks
along the underside of the front rail, leaving
5cm (2in) at each corner.

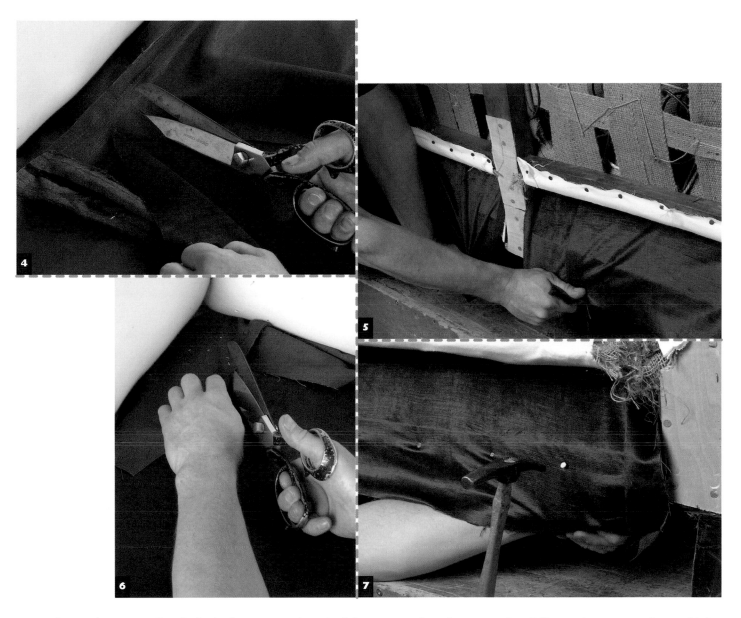

step 4 Locate the centre rail at the back of the sofa frame using your hands or a regulator. Fold the fabric back on itself over the seat and make a Y cut into it at the site of the centre rail so the fabric can be folded around it and pulled through. Be sure not to make the cut too deep.

step 5 Pull the fabric down either side of the centre rail and under the inside back rail making sure you are creating good tension across the seat.

step 6 In each of the corners, where the seat meets the inside back, fold the fabric back on itself as before and make a diagonal cut into the corner, then pull the fabric around each side of each back upright. Make a Y cut around each of the front upright rails and pull the fabric down and around these. If, like this sofa, the arm has an upright running down the centre, make a Y cut around this and again take the fabric down each side of this upright.

step 7 Place tacks to secure the top fabric to the base of the frame. You may wish to place temporary tacks initially until you are sure the fabric lies straight and has good tension and then hammer them home. Place spaced tacks along the back rail, leaving space around each corner and then tacks along each of the side rails, again leaving space around each of the corners. When placing the tacks, gently pull the fabric down so it lies taut across the length and width of the seat. Place more tacks along the underside of the front rail. Continue until the fabric is secure. Fold the fabric under around each corner so it lies snug against each upright rail and tack into place. Where the seat meets the front uprights secure the fabric to the upright with tacks (you can see this in place in the picture for step 9). Carefully trim away excess fabric.

step 8 Position the fabric for the inside arm and secure it with spaced tacks on the underside of the top arm rail.

step 9 Smooth the fabric over the top of the arm and down the inside to the seat. Make a Y cut in the fabric around the front upright.

step 10 Where the top of the arm meets the inside back make a Y cut and make another Y cut where the bottom of the arm meets the inside back. Carefully pull the fabric through around the back upright.

step 11 Take the fabric under the bottom arm rail, pulling it taut along the length of the arm, and secure it with spaced tacks along the side rail. At the back, tack the fabric down the length of the back upright.

Secure the fabric with tacks up the front upright and make a series of pleats around the scroll of the arm, securing these with tacks (see page 97 for further details on pleating an arm). Repeat steps 8–11 on the other arm.

step 12 Place the inside back panel over the back of the sofa, taking care to position it in the centre, smoothing it along the width and length of the inside back. Take the fabric over the top of the back and secure it along the head rail with spaced tacks. On the inside, again locate the upright centre rail, make a Y cut in the fabric around it, then pull the fabric down and around this rail. Continue to pull the fabric down and under the inside back rail, applying spaced tacks to the back rail.

step 13 Where the inside back meets the top of each arm, make a Y cut, and where the inside back meets the top of the seat make another Y cut. Pull the fabric through and around each back upright. Secure the fabric to each back upright, making sure it lies taut and smooth across the inside back. Around the curved sides of the inside back pull the fabric taut, making a series of small pleats, secure with tacks. Trim away excess fabric.

step 14 Move the sofa so you can easily access the underside of the outside arm, and place the fabric along the length of the arm, good side down, lining it up with the underside of the top arm rail. Initially place spaced tacks, gradually adding more. Attach a layer of hessian over the top fabric, followed by a length of back tacking strip. Both should be lined up with the underside of the top arm rail and secured with tacks. (Back tacking strip is purpose-made card that helps create a neat, straight edge along a tack line.) Pull the fabric down the outside arm and secure it under the side rail with a series of tacks. Where it meets the back leg, fold the fabric under and secure it under the side rail with a tack next to the leg.

step 15 Working the fabric as you go along, secure it around and onto the front upright and the back upright with spaced tacks, gradually adding more. Repeat steps 14 and 15 to make up the opposite arm.

step 16 Attach the outside back. Begin by placing the fabric over the inside back, good side facing down, so the top raw edge of the panel is lined up with the head rail on the outside back. Ensuring the fabric is lying straight, add spaced tacks to hold it in place. Add a layer of hessian. Next attach a length of back tacking strip along the straight part of the head rail. Take the fabric and hessian back over the head rail so they lie flat against the outside back.

step 17 At each of the outside back corners trim around the shape of the curve, leaving sufficient fabric to turn it under by 2cm (¾in). So the fabric will sit well around the inside of each curve, make a series of small cuts, then fold it under and secure with upholstery pins. Do not be too generous with the cuts. Continue to fold the fabric under down the length of each back upright.

step 18 Once both corners are pinned in place, attach the fabric to the underside of the back rail with temporary tacks, making sure the fabric sits well down the length of the outside back. Fold the fabric under around each of the back legs and secure it with a tack on the underside, close to the side of the leg.

step 19 Using a circular needle and slipping thread, slip stitch around each curve and down the sides. (See page 97, steps 14–16, for attaching fabric to the front arm facing.)

step 20 Trim away any excess fabric under the sofa. Cut sufficient dust cloth with a 5cm (2in) allowance all round and attach it to the underside of the sofa with four centre tacks, turning it under as you go. Gradually place more tacks along each side leaving space around the legs. Carefully cut around the shape of each leg and make neat folds to fit the cloth along each side; secure the folds with tacks, cutting away any excess fabric.

applying finishes and trimmings

Depending on their type, the various finishes and trimmings are added at different stages. For example, double piping, braid, gimp, and studs are always applied as the last stage of upholstering a piece of furniture, whereas single piping and flanged cord are machine-stitched between two panels of fabric, and sometimes tacked directly on to an item, so they are added at appropriate points throughout the upholstering process. A trimming or finish can have a big impact on the final appearance of a piece of furniture: piping accentuates curves and creates strong outlines, whereas braiding, often used to hide a tack line, produces a gentler effect. Take time to consider what is the most appropriate trimming for the item you are upholstering and how easy it will be to apply. (For ideas on the different types and styles, see pages 34–5.) As with top fabric, do not scrimp when ordering trimming materials, always err on the generous side.

tools
Craft knife, hot-glue gun, magnetic hammer, staple gun (optional), scissors, sewing machine.

materials
Gimp pins, glue sticks
piping cord, sewing machine thread,
10mm (⅜in) studs, 10mm (⅜in) tacks.

reference
Making single and double piping:
pp162–3.

applying studs

applying braid and ribbon

step 1 Decide on the colour and size of stud you are going to use and if you are going to close nail the studs (that is place them side by side) or space them apart. If you are studding a panel of leather or fabric to a chair, secure it with a few spaced tacks or similar coloured gimp pins first, this will help hold it in place while you are working on it. If you are placing spaced studs take care to put the tacks only where the studs will be going in.

step 2 Either begin in one corner and work your way around to the other side or begin in the centre at the top and work your way down one side and then down the other. Hold the stud between your thumb and forefinger, directly above where you want it to be, and hammer it on the head so it goes down in a straight line. If you hammer from an angle it will not go in straight and will look out of line. If you are attaching the studs next to each other, place them so the edges just touch each other. In general for spaced studs, a small finger's width apart looks good but bear in mind the size of the piece of furniture against the size of studs.

step 1 Cut sufficient braid or ribbon and add an allowance of 5cm (2in). In some cases, such as a (simple) dining chair, one length of braid or ribbon can be used to go around the whole chair, in other cases, several lengths may be required. Attach one end of the ribbon in the least obvious place on the chair, typically in the bottom of a corner or in the centre at the back. Make sure all the underlying fabric has been neatly trimmed and the glue gun is hot and ready for use.

step 2 Fold one end of the braid under itself and, applying the adhesive directly to the tack line, place the folded end on the tack line and hold it in place with a temporary tack.

applying double piping

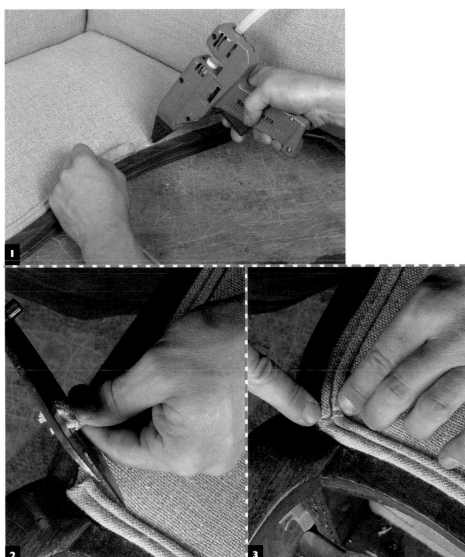

step 3 Continue applying adhesive very precisely along the tack line, pressing the braid down over the adhesive.

step 4 When working around a corner apply the adhesive directly to the braid to make it easier to position.

step 5 When you reach the point where you started, fold the loose end under so it sits snugly next to the first fold, and secure it in place with a temporary tack. Remove the tacks once the braid is securely glued.

step 1 Make up suitable lengths of piping to fit the relevant parts of the piece of furniture, adding an allowance of at least 10cm (4in) to each section of piping. Like braiding, begin by attaching the piping in the least conspicuous place on a chair: fold the end under itself and, using the hot-glue gun, attach this end to the chair, applying the glue directly to the tack line; hold the fold in place with a temporary tack. Continue to apply the glue carefully around the tack line, pressing the double piping down onto the adhesive as you go along.

step 2 When you return to the starting point, butt the two ends together. Cut open the unattached end of piping to reveal the cord. Trim it down so it will butt up against the first end.

step 3 Leave a little extra fabric at the end of the piping, so the fabric extends further than the cord. Fold this fabric under and attach with glue. Push the two ends together so they line up exactly with the start point and place a temporary tack securing the fold. Remove the tacks once the piping is stuck securely.

applying single piping directly

applying single piping to fabric

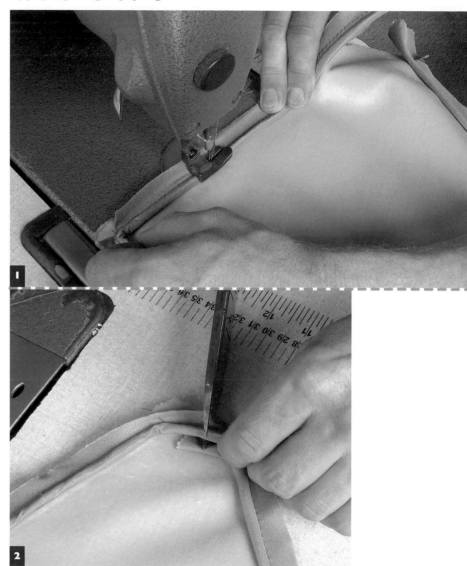

attaching piping directly onto a piece of furniture

step 1 Cut sufficient piping with a 5cm (2in) allowance at each end. Secure the piping in place – for example, along the length of the rail, such as the head rail or top arm rail – using tacks or staples. Take care to position it so it sits in a straight line, typically close to the top of a rail. Begin at one end of a rail and work to the other.

step 2 At corners, place a tack in the piping on the corner and take it around to commence the new direction. Cut a V shape out of the piping seam to make a neat corner. Continue along until the end of the rail and tack off, either to the underside of the chair or to a rail over which top fabric will be applied.

step 3 Attach the next panel of top fabric on the other side of the piping initially with tacks, followed by a back tacking strip, which will give a clean line against the piping (see applying top fabric, pages 68–71, and applying piping to the wing chair, page 120). The fabric should be attached so it fits snugly against the underside of the piping.

securing piping onto top fabric before it is attached to the piece of furniture

step 1 Cut the appropriate lengths of piping with an allowance of 5cm (2in) at each end. Using a sewing machine, attach the piping to the good side of the fabric panel with both raw edges aligned and sewing just below the piping to get a good fit. Begin at one end of the piece of fabric, leaving an allowance of at least 2cm (¾in) at the end of the piping, this will be used to butt the two ends together.

step 2 When you reach the point where you started, join the two ends neatly together. Cut open each end of piping to reveal the cord. Overlap the two pieces of cord so they lie side by side and then cut through both so they will butt together. Pin together the two ends of piping fabric where the two pieces of cord butt up and, using the sewing machine, make a seam on the bias (see page 162). Open out the seam, laying it flat, and trim away the excess. Wrap the fabric around the two ends of cord. Continue attaching the piping to the main panel of fabric as before.

making cushions

Cushions can make a significant contribution to the appearance and impact of a piece of furniture, adding subtle accents in different shapes, colours, and textures, or making strong statements in richer colours. They can also create a super-luxurious ambience, see page 94, or they can break up a plain fabric, providing interest, see page 98. Cushions can be used to unite the various colours in a room. The shape of the cushion will also have an effect; as well as box cushions, which are used for seats, there are bolsters, square, rectangular, or circular scatter cushions. There are many ways of being creative, such as combining several fabrics on one cushion or adding a whole choice of trimmings. Piping creates more definition around a cushion edge in comparison to a simple seam or a saddle stitch seam. Choose reasonably long zips for cushion covers as it is difficult trying to squash a cushion pad into a small opening. Use a pad that is fractionally larger than the cover (by about 1cm/⅜in) to ensure that the pad fits snugly, helping to maintain a good shape over time.

tools
Pins, scissors, sewing machine, tailor's chalk, tape measure.

materials
Piping cord, nylon zips, sewing machine thread.

reference
Applying single piping: p74, making single piping: p163.

scatter cushion

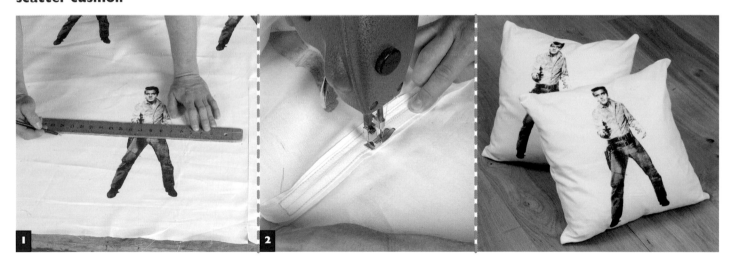

step 1 Mark up the cushion size on the fabric and cut out two panels with a 2cm (¾in) allowance all round. If the fabric you are using has a pattern or motif on it, take care that the pattern is positioned centrally.

step 2 Place one panel of fabric on top of the other, the good sides facing each other. Pin the panels together at their base with a 2cm (¾in) allowance, then machine sew along the pin line, stopping at the point where the zip will begin. Do the same from the other end – sewing to where the zip will end – thus leaving a long enough gap. Open

up the fabric so the panels lie face down with the seam flattened out on each side. Place the zip over the fabric so its teeth lie along the opening between the stitching and pin it in place. Using the zip foot on the sewing machine, attach the zip across its top end first, then sew down one side close to the teeth, continue over the zip end and sew back up the other side. If your sewing machine cannot sew over the ends of a nylon zip, do this by hand. Whether using a sewing machine or by hand, it is always good practice to go over each end twice to make it secure.

step 3 Pin together the rest of the cushion along the markings with the good sides facing in and machine stitch all the way around. Trim away a little of the fabric on the corners for a less bulky finish. Turn the cushion cover the right way out and carefully manipulate the cushion pad into it.

bolster cushion

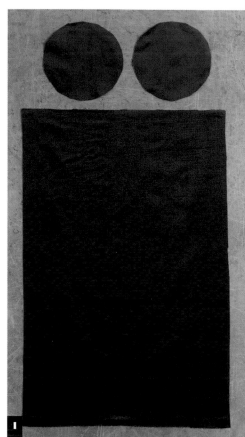

step 1 Measure the length and circumference of the cushion pad and use tailor's chalk to mark up the exact measurements on the reverse side of the fabric. Cut out each of the three panels of fabric with a 2cm (¾in) allowance all round.

step 2 Make sufficient single piping to go round each of the end panels, with an allowance of 5cm (2in). Position one end panel with the good side facing up, and lay the single piping beside it so both raw edges line up. Begin sewing the piping to the fabric, taking care to sew along the line of the chalk markings on the underside. As you work your way around, make small cuts in the hem to help it sit well. Where the two ends of piping meet, butt them together carefully (see page 74). Trim away any excess fabric. Attach single piping to the other end panel in the same way.

step 3 Take the panel of fabric for the body of the cushion and fold it in half lengthways with the good side of the fabric inside and lining up the raw edges. Sew the zip to the panel, using the method for attaching a zip in the scatter cushion (page 75).

step 4 Pin one of the end panels to one end of the main panel with the good side of the fabric facing in. Using the sewing machine, sew along the chalk markings, making sure the seam runs snugly against the piping seam. Trim away any excess fabric. Do the same with the other panel of fabric. Carefully turn the cushion cover the right way out and insert the cushion pad.

box cushion

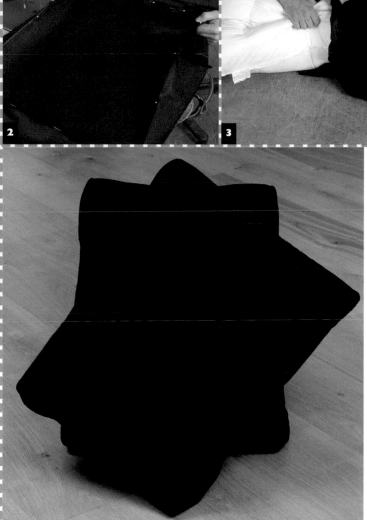

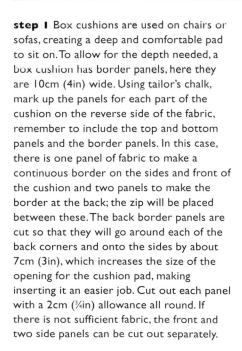

step 1 Box cushions are used on chairs or sofas, creating a deep and comfortable pad to sit on. To allow for the depth needed, a box cushion has border panels, here they are 10cm (4in) wide. Using tailor's chalk, mark up the panels for each part of the cushion on the reverse side of the fabric, remember to include the top and bottom panels and the border panels. In this case, there is one panel of fabric to make a continuous border on the sides and front of the cushion and two panels to make the border at the back; the zip will be placed between these. The back border panels are cut so that they will go around each of the back corners and onto the sides by about 7cm (3in), which increases the size of the opening for the cushion pad, making inserting it an easier job. Cut out each panel with a 2cm (¾in) allowance all round. If there is not sufficient fabric, the front and two side panels can be cut out separately.

step 2 Attach the zip to the back border panels in the same way as for the scatter cushion (page 75). The zip can go around the back corners, with the panels if desired, making the opening larger. Attach the back border panel to each end of the main border panel with a 2cm (¾in) hem, pinning it first and then sewing it. Now pin and sew the top panel to the main border and back panel. Start with the back panel, sew around one side, then the front, then the second side, coming back to where you started. Make a 2cm (¾in) hem, following the markings you made when drawing up the panels. At each corner, make a mark on the bottom of the

border, this is to make sure the corners on the bottom panel of fabric correspond to the corners on the top panel. Attach the bottom panel, ensuring when you pin it together that the corner markings line up.

step 3 Trim away any excess fabric and turn the cushion cover the right way out. Manipulate the cushion pad into the cover, squeezing it together to help it go in.

upholstered furniture

pair of salon chairs

This elegant pair of salon chairs, circa early twentieth century, have graceful shaped legs at the back and front and ornate carvings on the chair back. The black lacquer that has been applied at some stage in the chairs' history lends them a rather glamorous appearance. To complement this, the fabric chosen to cover them is opulent with a cream background and black flock print. The velvet flock works particularly well with the carving. For the trimming a simple band of black velvet has been chosen to set off the chair's black paint finish and the black flocking on the fabric. As it is plain, the trimming will neither distract from or fight with the top fabric. With a chair like this you will be working very close to the show wood, so take care when applying the tacks; you may wish to use a staple gun instead.

tools
Craft knife, hot-glue gun, magnetic hammer, pins, scissors, staple gun (optional).

materials
Adhesive sticks, piping, 13mm (½in) tacks, top fabric.

reference
Over-stuffed seat pad such as this: 48–52, applying piping: pp72–4, cuts, corners, and folds: pp158–9, stitches: pp160–63.

step 1 Prepare the chair to the calico stage: strip back the chair, apply webbing followed by a base layer of hessian. Make a series of bridle ties, add the stuffing, and secure it. Add another layer of hessian and create a firm seat with a row of wall stitches and a row of roll stitch around the pad's top edge. Sew some through stitches in the pad, then add a second layer of stuffing to fill out any dips in the centre of the pad. Now position a layer of cotton felt and, finally, apply the calico.

step 2 Cut the top fabric with a 10cm (4in) allowance all round. Lay the fabric on the seat pad, taking care to position it so the pattern lies straight and to its best advantage. Secure the fabric by placing a temporary tack in the centre of each side rail. Fold the fabric back from each back upright and make a T cut, stopping a minimum of 2cm (¾in) from the upright. If the cut is made too close, the fabric may tear around the corners.

step 3 Carefully fold the fabric around and down each side of the upright, smoothing it into position, trimming away any excess fabric from within the fold. Repeat on the other upright.

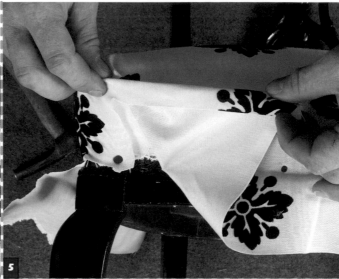

step 4 Secure the fabric around the frame with tacks. Manipulating the fabric into position, place a series of spaced tacks around the frame, stopping 5cm (2in) from the corners and taking care not to damage the show wood beneath the fabric (you may prefer to use a staple gun for attaching the fabric instead). Take care to work around the earlier tacks placed to secure the calico. Ease the fabric onto the tack line – the neater the tacks are around the edges, the cleaner the end result when the trimming is in place. Work the fabric across the seat pad, making sure the grain lies straight and taut. Now hammer home in the initial centre tacks.

step 5 Attach the fabric around the front corners. First smooth the excess fabric at the corner around from the side of the seat to the front and place a tack to secure it. Next trim away the excess fabric at the corner to reduce its bulk. Now fold the raw edge under and smooth the fabric back down over the front edge of the seat to create a neat vertical line down the length of the corner.

step 6 Holding the fold in place, attach a tack to secure it. Repeat on the other front corner. Place the remaining tacks around the corners to complete the tacking process. Trim away the excess fabric using a craft knife, taking care not to mark the show wood.

step 7 To apply the trimming, begin by attaching the band along the back rail, starting at the centre. Using the hot-glue gun, add some glue to one end of the trimming and attach this to the centre of the rail, turning it under. Apply pressure and then temporarily secure it with a pin. Continue attaching the trimming along the back rail to the first upright. Carefully fold the trimming to enable it to change direction to go up and around the back upright, and securing the fold temporarily with a pin.

step 8 When applying the glue around the back corner of the seat pad, take care to make a clean line of glue exactly where you wish the velvet to be fixed. Position it around the back upright, gently pushing it into place with your finger.

step 9 Continue fixing the trimming along the sides of the frame, applying pressure as you go, and carefully manoeuvring around corners as in step 7.

step 10 At the centre back of the frame, where you reach the beginning of the trimming, create a neat finish by folding the end under. Make sure the fold butts up to the first fold exactly with no space in between or an overlap.

step 11 Attach the dust cloth to the base of the chair; in this case it is hessian. Cut enough hessian to cover the base with a 10cm (4in) allowance all round. Attach it to the underside of the seat frame with four centre tacks, turning it under by 2cm (¾in). Apply spaced tacks out from the centre, stopping 5cm (2in) away from each corner.

step 12 At the corners, make a T cut in towards the centre of each leg. Fold the excess hessian under around the chair leg and place a tack on each side to secure it.

arts and crafts side chair

The simplicity and fluid lines of this Arts and Crafts chair make it a charming and rather unusual piece of furniture. As the chair has a simple and elegant character, a fine and not too elaborate fabric was chosen to complement it. This rich green silk fabric is very effective as the gentle lines of the velvet leaf flock echo the flowing lines of the wooden batons that make up the chair back and legs. Although covering the chair seat is a fairly simple exercise, it is important to take time placing the fabric to ensure it sits perfectly within the wooden frame, and that the studs are evenly spaced. Silk (in conjunction with a barrier cloth) has been used here as the chair is intended for decorative purposes only. This project focuses on how to apply top fabric to a top-stuffed seat (see reference, opposite).

tools
Craft knife, magnetic hammer, scissors, staple gun (optional).

materials
13mm (½in) antique finish studs, 10mm (⅜in) gimp pins, top fabric.

reference
Top stuffing: pp45–7, applying studs: p72.

step 1 Cut sufficient top fabric, allowing for a 2cm (¾in) hem all round. If you are working with a pattern, consider where the pattern will lie on the seat pad, bearing in mind this seat is relatively small.

step 2 Place the fabric over the barrier cloth making sure it lies straight. On one side, carefully fold under the fabric with a 2cm (¾in) hem and place the fold just inside the lip of the wooden frame, along the edge of the barrier cloth. Temporarily secure this in place in the centre of the rail using a matching gimp pin. Do the same thing on the other side of the frame and then along the back and the front of the seat pad. Once you are happy with how the fabric lies and you have achieved the correct tension across the seat pad, hammer home the centre gimp pins.

step 3 Carefully fold under the fabric around each corner, trimming away some of the excess for neatness. Make a simple fold, turning one hem under the other. Take care the fabric lies flat at all times, so that when you secure each corner there are no rucks. Secure each corner fold with a gimp pin.

step 4 Place the studs evenly along the four edges of the seat pad. You may wish to work out the exact spacing between each stud in relation to the dimensions of the pad, or simply space them about a finger-width apart. Place the first stud on top of one of the centre gimp pins and then, holding down the fabric with your thumb, apply the next stud. Work your way from each centre, out towards the corners. Take time to fit the fabric exactly so it sits just inside the lip of the wooden frame and is smooth and flat.

balloon-back dining chair

This nineteenth century balloon-back dining chair has a drop-in seat pad; these are wonderfully straightforward to reupholster. When this chair was found, the mahogany needed a good polishing and there was a bad split on the lower side of the balloon. Don't be put off a piece of furniture if it has a split like this, often the worst-looking damage is the easiest to fix. Only a hairline crack was left once the wood restorer had finished, and the cost of the repair did not break the bank. Mahogany is a very rich and lustrous wood that gains in character over the years. This character is complemented here by the choice of top fabric: the sumptuous texture of the dark hair on the pony skin creates an intriguing contrast to the rich patina of the wood (an effect which equally could be created with a black velvet or other rich fabric). During the reupholstering process, special attention is required at the rear corners where the back uprights cut into the pad's frame. It is also important to reduce any bulk in stuffing and fabric so that it fits neatly back on the chair.

tools
Circular needle, craft knife, magnetic hammer, scissors, staple gun (optional).

materials
Calico, clear plastic card, cotton felt, fibre, hessian, masking tape, top fabric, stitching twine, 13mm (½in) tacks.

reference
Applying webbing: pp42–3, applying base hessian: p44, cuts, corners, and folds: pp158–9, stitches: pp160–3 (bridle ties: p162).

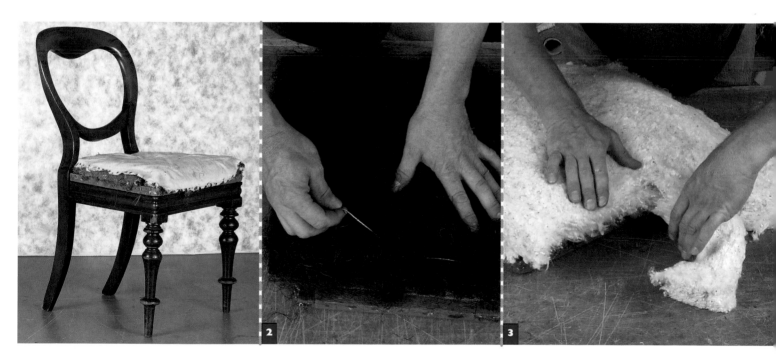

step 1 The stuffing on this pad was rather old and worn out so it needed rebuilding from scratch. Attach three strips of webbing lengthways and from side to side. Attach them to the top of the pad frame as there are no springs on this seat. Add a layer of hessian over the webbing, then make a series of bridle ties in the hessian, taking care to stitch through the hessian only.

step 2 Tuck the stuffing under the bridle ties. Use plenty of fibre as it will be compressed when the calico is put in place. Tease out any lumps in the fibre as you go, ensuring there is an even spread of stuffing over the pad. Pull the bridle ties in to hold the stuffing in place.

step 3 Take enough cotton felt to cover the pad easily. Position it over the stuffing and hold it down with one hand, gently tearing away the excess from around the pad frame with the other, so that the edges are just inside the rim.

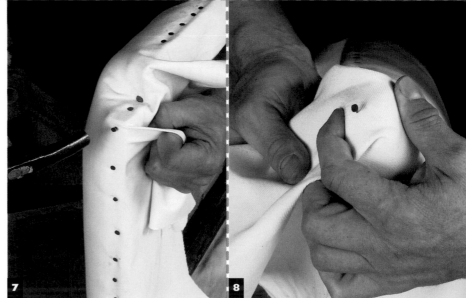

step 4 Cut a piece of calico with an allowance of 12cm (4¾in) all round and place this over the cotton felt. Place four temporary tacks at the centre of each side, on the edge of the frame. Take care to pull the calico across the pad, helping to secure the stuffing and cotton felt underneath and always making sure the weave of the fabric is lying straight. Place spaced tacks along each side of the frame, stopping 5cm (2in) away from the corners.

step 5 Pull the calico across the pad towards the back corners. As you pull it round the corners, check that none of the stuffing is being dragged into the corner shaping. If it is, trim it back to ensure that the pad will eventually fit back snugly in place around the back uprights.

step 6 Pull the calico into the recessed corner and hold in place with a tack on each side of the recess.

step 7 Pull the calico down and into place on each side of the frame next to the recess and place a tack to hold in place. Continue the tacks along the side edge up to the corner. Repeat the process on the other back corner.

step 8 Secure the front corners by pulling the calico taut over the corner and place one tack on each side of the corner. Take the excess calico from each side of the corner across to the base of the corner creating two neat diagonal folds and secure with a tack on each side. Repeat this process on the other front corner. Use a craft knife to trim off the excess calico along the edge of the frame just under the tacks, reducing the bulk as much as possible.

step 9 Measure the pony skin, adding an allowance of 7cm (3in) all round. Mark out the piece of hide from the top side so that you can see and avoid any imperfections, such as branding marks, small holes, or scratches. A large piece of clear plastic card (available from most stationery or craft shops) is useful to make a pattern through which to see the hide underneath, and masking tape is the best way to mark the area you need to cut. It is easy to apply and reapply and also helps reduce the amount of hair that falls away once you start cutting.

step 10 Attach the pony skin in the same way as the calico, including at the back corners, except this time fold and tack the skin to the underneath of the frame. At the front corners, tack the side edge in place right up to the corner. Then trim the excess skin at the corner to reduce bulk and tack the overlap from the side to the front of the frame. Fold the excess skin from the front underneath to make a vertical line down the corner and tack securely under the frame. Repeat the process on the other front corner. With fabric, be sure to check the weave lies straight; with pony skin, really stretch it across the pad as, like leather, the

hide will give over time. Pony skin creates greater thickness so again, particularly around the corners, it needs to be pulled in tight, making the folds as slim as possible.

step 11 Trim away the excess pony skin on the underside of the frame, close to the tacks. Also trim around any peg holes so that the pegs will easily slip back into them. This seat frame has two peg holes, which accommodate the pegs on the chair frame holding the top and bottom frames together.

step 12 Cut the dust cloth: here we are using hessian, with a 5cm (2in) allowance all round. Place four centre tacks, one on the underside of each edge of the frame, tucking the material under with a 2cm (¾in) hem. Turn the corners in at the front, place tacks either side, and trim away the excess lip. Trim around the back corners, turning the hessian under, and place tacks around the corner. Complete the tacking at 1cm (½in) intervals along all the edges. The drop-in seat pad is now complete.

arts and crafts easy chair

This Arts and Crafts oak chair was found with its original fabric still intact. Years of polishing with a dark polish had left the wood dull and sombre, but stripping it back and repolishing it by hand produced a rich waxed finish through which the oak grain was visible once again. The main features of this chair are the simplicity and boldness of the arms and the abundance of wood – this unusual, textured, geometric silk in cream and brown was chosen to enhance these characteristics. Although beautiful, silk is suitable for light domestic or decorative use only as it is a more delicate and less durable fabric. A fire retardant barrier cloth is used in place of calico. As there is so much show wood on this chair, care is needed when tacking the various layers. A staple gun may be preferable for such a project.

tools
Craft knife, hot-glue gun, magnetic hammer, pins, scissors, staple gun (optional).

materials
Adhesive sticks, barrier cloth, cotton felt, hessian, 13mm (½in) tacks, top fabric.

reference
Applying piping: pp72–4, cuts, corners, and folds: pp158–9, applying a dust cloth: p83.

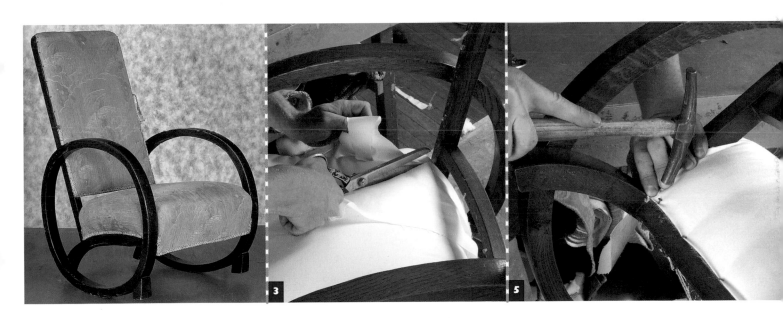

step 1 The stuffing in the seat was in good condition, so only new cotton felt and barrier cloth were applied, along with the top fabric. Remove the top fabric and the old layer of cotton felt. Apply a new layer of cotton felt, tearing it away just above the base tack line. Remember that the barrier cloth will bring the cotton felt closer to the tack line.

step 2 Cut the barrier cloth for the seat with a 10cm (4in) allowance and secure it. Place a centre tack on the top of the back and side rails and under the front rail. Check that the shape of the seat is good and that the cloth is straight and has reasonable tension, then apply spaced tacks along the frame from the centre tacks towards the corners, stopping 5cm (2in) away from each corner.

step 3 To work the barrier cloth around the back uprights, peel the cloth back towards the centre of the chair and make a T cut into the centre corner of one back upright. Do not cut right up to the wood; stop 2cm (¾in) away. Fold the cloth neatly and firmly down either side of the upright, place a tack on either side, and trim away the excess flaps of cloth. Repeat on the other upright.

step 4 Make T cuts around each of the front arm uprights, folding the barrier cloth around and down each side of the uprights, securing each fold with a tack.

step 5 Apply spaced tacks, approximately 1.5cm (½in) apart, along the top of the side and back rails, continually checking that the tension on the cloth is good and that the weave lies straight. Tack the front edge in place underneath the front rail. Trim away the excess cloth.

step 6 Start rebuilding and recovering the chair back. As the fabric for the outside back can be seen through the wooden frame, begin by applying this. Measure enough top fabric to fit, with an additional 5cm (2in) allowance all round. With patterned fabric, work out the pattern repeat so that the piece used for the outside back of the chair continues the pattern on from, in this case, the pattern on the back of the seat.

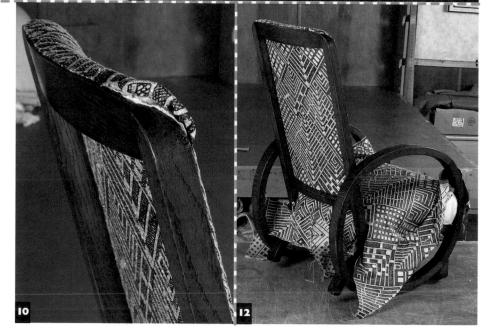

step 7 Attach the top fabric to the top of the inside back frame with four centre tacks, one along each side, making a 2cm (¾in) hem, turning the fabric over rather than under. As this is the fabric that will be seen from behind remember to have the wrong side of the fabric facing you as you work. Creating a good tension with the fabric across the frame, apply tacks along the top, working towards the corners, but leaving a space around them. Apply tacks to the bottom of the frame, again working towards the corners. Then tack along both side rails. Finally, place tacks around the corners, taking care there are no wrinkles in the fabric. Trim away the excess fabric with a craft knife.

step 8 Place a layer of hessian over the top of the top fabric, attaching it in the same way. Follow this with a layer of cotton felt and then a layer of barrier cloth. Cut the barrier cloth with a 2.5cm (1in) allowance all round, turn it under the cotton felt, and tack it in the same order as for the top fabric (step 7). Take care over the corners.

step 9 Cut the top fabric for the inside back with a 5cm (2in) allowance, again considering the pattern in relation to the seat. It will need to follow on from the pattern at the top of the back edge of the seat (from the front you will not see the fabric that goes down the back of the chair seat). Place a centre tack on each of the top and bottom rails and each upright, turning the fabric under. Tack the fabric in place along the bottom and side rails, again turning it under, working from the centre tacks towards the corners, leaving space at the corners. Place temporary tacks first and hammer them home when you are sure the fabric lies perfectly. If you prefer,

use a staple gun. Staples lie flatter and will cause less damage to the surrounding wood. Trim a little of the fabric away at the bottom corners so they do not become too bulky with the various layers underneath but leave enough to turn under.

step 10 At the top, take the fabric over to the back edge of the top rail before securing it. Trim and fold under the excess fabric on each corner, then tack the fabric, turning it under, working out from the centre tack and along the edge to the corners. Trim away the excess fabric close to the tack line.

step 11 Cut the top fabric for the seat with an allowance of 10cm (4in), ensuring that the pattern will line up with that on the inside back.

step 12 Place a centre tack on the top of the side and back rails and one on the underside of the front rail. Apply more spaced tacks leaving a 5cm (2in) gap around the corners. Make a T cut into the back uprights to within 2cm (¾in) of the corners.

step 13 Pull the fabric down and create a neat fold either side of the back uprights. Secure it with a tack on top of the side and back rail and trim away the flaps of fabric.

step 14 Make a T cut into the front uprights to within 2cm (¾in) of the corners. Pull the fabric down either side of the uprights and underneath the front rail. Tack the fabric in place along the underside of the front rail and along the top of the side rails.

step 15 Trim away the fabric close to the tack line on the back and side rails and underneath the front rail, using a craft knife. Work away from you and work carefully so as not to damage the show wood.

step 16 Apply the trimming, which will hide the tack line. Here, a very simple piece of brown, ready-made double piping is used. Alternatively, double piping could be made using the silk fabric. Measure all around the bottom edge of the chair seat and all round the inside chair back, and cut two pieces of piping each with a 5cm (2in) allowance.

step 17 Begin by attaching the piping to the seat. Take one end of the piping and secure it to the underside of the front of the chair directly beneath and in line with the left front upright. Secure it here with two tacks and then, using the hot glue gun, take it up and around the upright, carefully

fitting it around the corner and down the other side. Continue along the left side rail, continually pressing it firmly in place, around the back upright and around the back of the seat. Carry on until you reach the right front upright and secure the end with two tacks to the underside of the front seat.

step 18 Now attach the piping to the inside back. Apply some adhesive at one end of the piping, turn it under and press it firmly in place in the centre of the bottom

of the frame. Temporarily secure the end with a pin. Pressing the piping firmly in place continue along to the first bottom corner and mould it smoothly around the shape. At the first top corner, follow the edge of fabric around on to the back edge of the top back rail in a smooth curve. When you reach the start point again, turn the piping under and glue it firmly in place, holding the join temporarily with a pin. When the adhesive has dried, remove all the pins. Finally, attach the dust cloth to the underside of the chair.

sofa

Sofas can appear daunting due to their size, but they are not necessarily the most complicated pieces to upholster. This is a relatively plain late nineteenth-century sofa, but in terms of shape and proportions, it is somewhat grand. The proportions of the arms are generous, creating wonderful curves and the sofa back, although simple, is gently rounded at each end, softening the overall shape and giving the piece an elegant outline. The plain shape provides an excellent opportunity to use an opulent fabric in a luxurious dark smoky pink with a pile that emphasizes the curves of the sofa by catching the light. The sumptuous elegance is taken further by using an abundance of cushions in crushed claret-red velvet and deep pink satin. These fabrics work well together as each comes from the same colour family. Interest is added by the different textures of the silk, plain velvet, and satin and velvet flock. This project focuses on how to build up an arm using a panel of springs. (To learn more about attaching top fabric to a sofa, see page 68.)

tools
Craft knife, double-ended needle, magnetic hammer, scissors, skewers, spring needle, web strainer.

materials
Calico, cotton felt, hessian, panel of springs, piping cord, stitching twine, stuffing, 13mm (½in) tacks, top fabric, webbing.

reference
Applying webbing: pp42–3, applying hessian: p44, over stuffing: pp48–52, springing: p53–6, cuts, corners, and folds: pp158–9, stitches: pp160–3, applying piping: p74, pleating: p158.

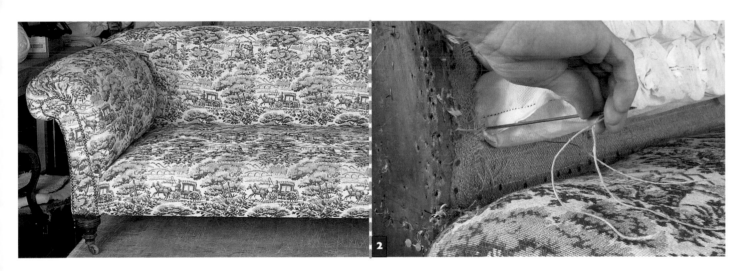

step 1 When this sofa was originally upholstered, a panel of springs was used on each of arms instead of single springs, to save time. The whole panel now needs to be replaced. Carefully remove the top fabric. Now remove the panel of springs as a unit by cutting the twine holding them to the hessian underneath. Check to see if the webbing and hessian under the springs are still intact, if not, apply eight strips of webbing from the top of the arm to the bottom arm rail. Next add two wide strips of webbing from the front upright to the back upright, weaving them through the vertical strips to make a strong platform for the springs.

step 2 Use the old panel of springs as a guideline for the number of new springs needed and where they will sit on the arm. Place the new set of springs over the arm so they sit along the top of the top arm rail, about 8cm (3in) above the seat and 8cm (3in) in from the front arm upright; they should fit close to the inside back. Hold the springs in place along the top arm rail with four tacks in the fabric of the panel. Then, using a double-ended needle and stitching

twine, begin by attaching the springs at the base near the front arm rail. Fasten the twine with a slip knot and then make a series of stitches to work your way around the set of springs, securing the base of each spring to the hessian and webbing underneath. Tie off each spring by wrapping the twine around the needle twice before moving on to the next.

step 3 Add stuffing between each row of springs on the panel. This gives more body to the shape and separates the springs, helping to keep them in place. Carefully prise apart each row, adding a good amount of stuffing in between.

step 4 Add a layer of hessian to further secure the springs. Cut sufficient hessian with a 10cm (4in) allowance all round. Place four centre tacks to secure it initially: one on the outside of the top arm rail, one on the inside of the front upright, one on the underside of the bottom arm rail, and one on the back upright. Cut around each of the uprights and place spaced tacks to secure the hessian. Where the hessian lies along the top of the arm rail and down the front arm upright, turn it over with a 2cm (¾in) hem and tack this down.

step 5 Sew the springs to the hessian using a spring needle and stitching twine. Make a slip knot at the start and then attach every other spring (see pages 53–6 for further details on attaching springs).

step 6 Make a series of bridle ties in the hessian and tuck stuffing under them. Ensure the stuffing is evenly placed, teasing out any lumps along the way. Apply a good amount of stuffing, taking particular care around the curve on the front upright.

step 7 Place a layer of hessian over the stuffing, taking it around the top of the arm and attaching it to the underside of the top arm rail, to the back upright, the underside of the bottom arm rail, and along the edge of the front upright. Using a regulator, bring some of the stuffing to the front edge of the arm. To create a firm edge around the front of the arm, place one row of wall stitch followed by one row of roll stitch (see pages 48–50 and 160–1). Start these from the base of the front upright, working around to the underside of the top arm rail.

step 8 Add another layer of stuffing over the hessian, to fill out any dips created by pulling the stuffing to the front edge, then add two layers of cotton felt to help shape the arm. Take these over the top of the arm and tuck them between the arm and the seat.

step 9 Cut enough calico with a 10cm (4in) allowance all round and attach it with tacks to the centre of the bottom arm rail, the centre of the back upright, and the centre of the top arm rail, and then use one tack on the face of the front upright, placing it at the bottom. At the front of the arm, pull the calico around the top of the arm rail and around the curve, and place a tack at the top of the front upright. Continue to attach the calico with spaced tacks, working it as you go along, ensuring the weave lies straight. Aim to create a firm, rounded shape on which to place the top fabric.

step 10 Work the calico around the curve at the front of the arm by pulling it across and making a series of single pleats. Work from the outside of the curve on each side in towards the centre top and secure each pleat as it is made with a tack. The tacks should sit just inside the curve on the facing of the wooden front upright, so there will be less bulk when the pleats on the top fabric are made (you need to leave as much space as possible for the subsequent layer of tacks). Ensure that the calico is taut as you pull it into the curve. Trim away the excess. Place spaced tacks to secure the calico down the front of the arm upright.

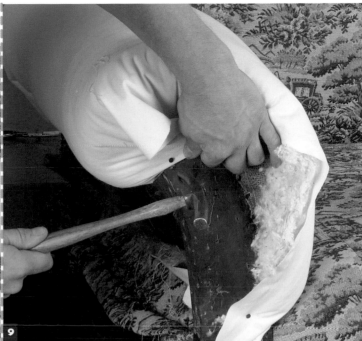

step 11 Prepare the rest of the sofa to calico stage and apply the top fabric to the sofa seat (see pages 68–9, steps 2–11).

step 12 Attach the top fabric to the arm in the same way as the calico. This fabric has a pile that must lie in the right direction (when you stroke the fabric in a downwards direction the pile lies flat and feels smooth). To make the first pleat, start in the centre, pulling the fabric out and then down and secure with a tack. Now make a pleat to each side of this. Pull each pleat tightly into the centre of the arm facing so that it lies flat; ensure each pleat is a similar size so the end result looks balanced. Continue to attach the fabric down the length of the arm facing with tacks.

step 13 Attach the top fabric to the inside back and then the outside arms (see pages 70–1, steps 12–19).

step 14 Prepare the piping to go around the front arm facing. When making the piping, leave a fabric hem of about 2cm (¾in). Beginning at the base of the arm facing and leaving the small amount over to attach the piping to the underside of the frame, place a tack in the hem of the piping, making sure it is snug where it meets the edge of the seat. Continue to place tacks in a

straight line up the arm facing, taking care at the top to create a good clean curve around the base of the pleats. Continue down the outside of the arm facing until you reach the bottom, then turn the corner, placing a tack in the corner to secure it, and bring the piping along the bottom of the arm facing. Neatly butt this end against the start point and then secure the other end to the underside of the frame.

step 15 Cut top fabric in the shape of the arm facing with a 2.5cm (1in) allowance all round. Turning it under, carefully skewer the fabric into place inside the line of piping. Make a series of small cuts to the fabric to help ease it around the inside of the curve.

step 16 Use a circular needle to secure the arm facing fabric with slip stitching. Finally, attach the outside back fabric (see page 71) and apply a dust cloth.

button-back chair

This elegant early twentieth-century button-back chair has a metal frame back and arms and a wooden frame seat, which is typical of the period. It is particularly comfortable as the stuffing is not too pronounced and the seat is deep and wide. In order not to distract from the shape of the chair and the buttoning, a plain wool fabric was chosen, which also lends it a more contemporary look. This is enhanced by the small cushion with its luxuriously soft faux fur cover creating another dimension and providing a delicate contrast to the wool. Plain fabric is a lot easier to use for deep buttoning, especially if it is your first attempt, as there is no problem with matching up the patterns. With a patterned fabric, more material is needed, and you must plan very carefully the position of the pattern in relation to the buttons, the folds, and the seat fabric. Machines that cover buttons are very expensive so it is worth asking a local upholsterer to do this for you.

tools
Circular slipping needle, chalk, craft knife, double-ended needle, large circular needle, magnetic hammer, pins, skewers, scissors, tape measure, wood rule.

materials
Buttoning twine, 13mm (½in) buttons (covered in top fabric), calico, cotton felt, gimp pins, hessian, slipping thread, stitching twine, skin wadding, 13mm (½in) tacks, top fabric, upholstery thread.

reference
Cuts, corners, folds, stitches, and knots: pp158–164, applying a dust cloth: p83, deep buttoning: p60.

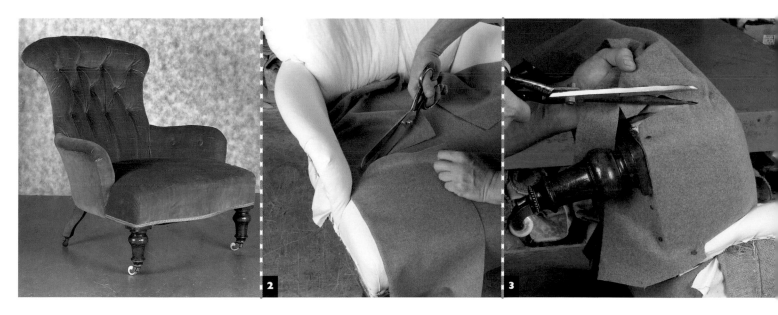

step 1 Overall this chair was in good condition, needing only a new layer of cotton felt on the seat and arms, and cotton felt and skin wadding on the inside back. Remove the top fabric. Cut the twine to release the buttons. Remove the old cotton felt and apply a new layer: on the seat, tuck it down the sides and back by at least 2.5cm (1in); on the inside back, take it just around the sides and top of the frame and down to the seat; follow the contours of the arms, gently pulling it away around them. Now apply skin wadding to the inside back. Re-cover the seat in calico, attaching it with tacks and trimming away the excess. Leave the bottom edge of calico on the inside arms unattached.

step 2 Cut the top fabric for the seat with an extra 10cm (4in) all round. Place it on the seat, ensuring it lies smoothly and that the weave is straight. Make a straight cut at right angles in towards each front upright and a T cut to each back upright. Cut to within 2.5cm (1in) of each upright. This chair has an upright in the centre of each arm rail and one in the centre of the back rail. Make a Y cut around each of these rails and pull the fabric around them and between the seat and the inside panels on all sides.

step 3 Attach the fabric with three temporary tacks to the outside centre of the back rail and three spaced tacks on the underside of the front rail. Make a straight cut in the fabric at the back of the front leg, take the fabric under the frame, and secure it with two tacks. Place a tack on the side rail just below the front upright. Take the fabric around the corner to the front of the seat frame, folding it under to create a neat line along the top edge of the leg, and place a tack. Cut away some of the excess fabric, pull the rest across to the corner, and fold it under to create a neat vertical line at the corner of the seat.

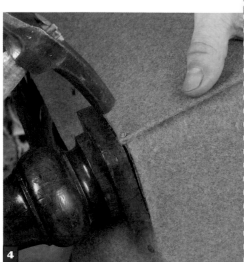

step 4 Carefully fold the fabric under at the base of the seat to lie flush with the top of the front chair leg and secure it with a gimp pin.

step 5 This is quite a long fold, so slip stitch it in place to stop it from coming loose in the future. Begin at the top of the seam, securing the thread with a slip knot, and work your way down, making neat, even stitches. Secure the thread at the bottom with a locking knot.

step 6 Measure fabric for the arms, being sure to allow for the curve at their top, and cut it with 10cm (4in) extra all around. Position the fabric on the arm. Make a Y cut around the front arm upright and a T cut towards the back upright and pull the fabric down and around each upright. Also make a Y cut around the upright in the centre of the arm and pull the fabric down and under the bottom arm rail.

step 7 Smooth the fabric over the top edge of the arm and temporarily secure it along the top of the outside arm with skewers.

step 8 Pull the fabric taut around the curve on the front of the arm, ensuring you are pulling it across as well as down, and secure it with a skewer. Now make pleats around the corner of the arm. Pull down the fabric around the middle of the corner, then fold over the fabric from the top of the arm to make one pleat, and fold over the fabric from the side of the arm to create another.

step 9 Secure the pleats with a slip knot and a few stitches. The fabric at the back end of the arm where it meets the outside back is secured at a later stage (see steps 17 and 18). Repeat steps 6 to 9 on the other arm, making sure the two arms match each other.

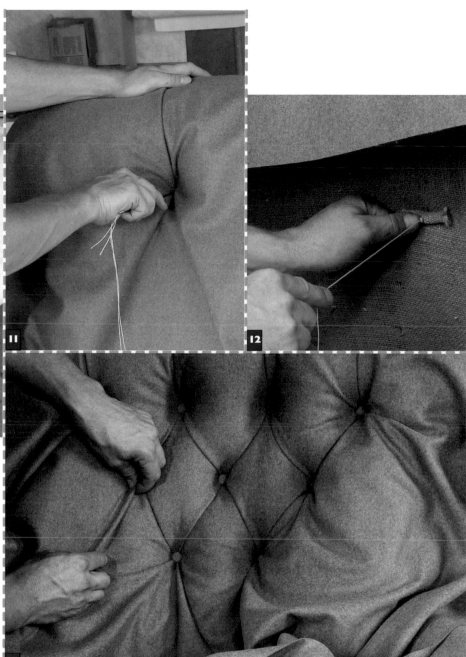

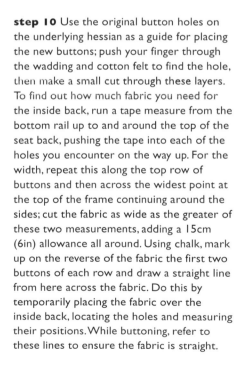

step 10 Use the original button holes on the underlying hessian as a guide for placing the new buttons; push your finger through the wadding and cotton felt to find the hole, then make a small cut through these layers. To find out how much fabric you need for the inside back, run a tape measure from the bottom rail up to and around the top of the seat back, pushing the tape into each of the holes you encounter on the way up. For the width, repeat this along the top row of buttons and then across the widest point at the top of the frame continuing around the sides; cut the fabric as wide as the greater of these two measurements, adding a 15cm (6in) allowance all around. Using chalk, mark up on the reverse of the fabric the first two buttons of each row and draw a straight line from here across the fabric. Do this by temporarily placing the fabric over the inside back, locating the holes and measuring their positions. While buttoning, refer to these lines to ensure the fabric is straight.

step 11 Lay the fabric over the chair and, on the top row of button holes, locate one of the middle holes, pushing the fabric in with your finger. Thread a covered button with a long length of twine and then thread both ends of the twine onto the buttoning

needle. Push the needle into the fabric, taking it right through to the outside back.

step 12 Take a small piece of folded hessian and thread this on to the twine at the back of the frame, pulling it tight against the frame and securing it with a double slip knot, followed by two single knots.

step 13 Continue placing buttons along the top row, making folds in the fabric along the top of the frame. Stitch the buttons into place on the second row, again taking care to make a fold in the fabric above as you go, thus creating the beginnings of a diamond shape. Repeat this process on the third row of buttons, creating neat, symmetrical diamond shapes. Keep checking that the fabric remains straight along the seat back.

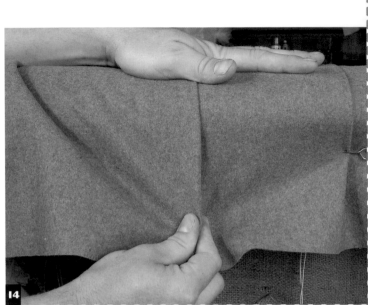

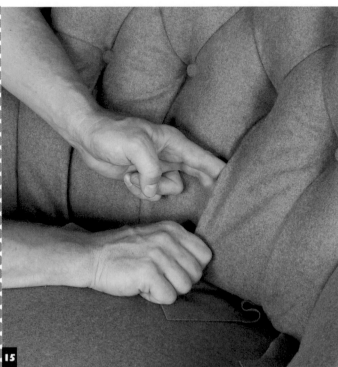

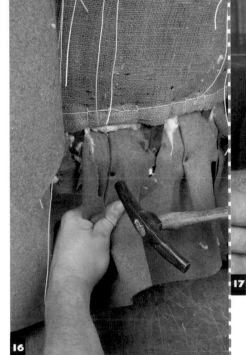

step 14 Neaten the folds that run from each button in the top row over the top of the chair. Use skewers to secure them to the chair back.

step 15 Create a series of neat folds from each of the buttons in the bottom row down to the base of the inside back and tuck the fabric behind the seat to the top of the back rail, making a Y cut where the fabric meets the centre back upright. Make a T cut towards each back upright.

step 16 Pull the fabric down between the seat and the inside back, around each of the uprights, and secure each fold with a tack on the bottom rail.

step 17 Secure the fabric for the inside back and inside arms around the frame. As this is metal, this is not done with tacks; instead, hold it in place with skewers and then permanently secure it with a series of blanket stitches, which help to draw the fabric tighter. Begin by folding the inside back fabric under where it meets the top of the inside arm and place a skewer to hold this fold. Smooth the rest of the fabric around the frame and secure it with more skewers, making small cuts where necessary so that it lies flat around the curves.

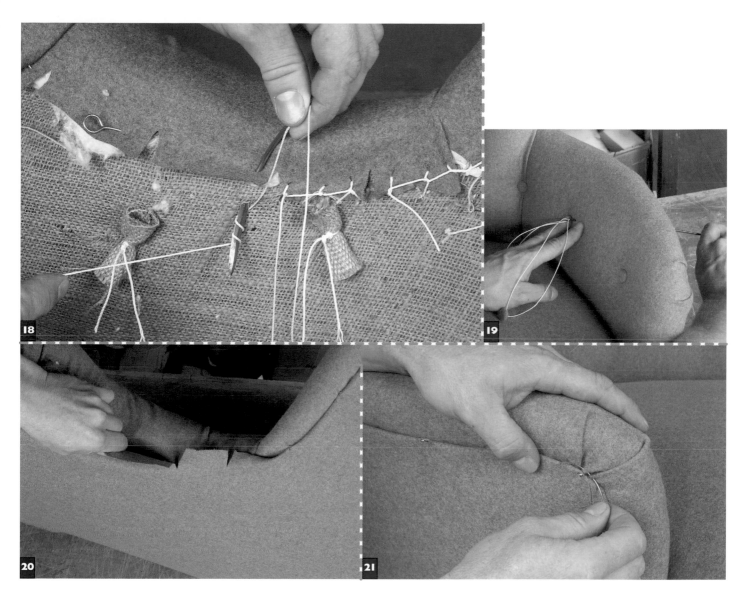

step 18 Begin the blanket stitches at the base of one outside arm, working your way up and along it, then up and around the outside back, and along the other arm. Start and finish each length of twine with a slip knot and end with a single knot.

step 19 Attach three "blind" buttons to the inside of each arm: two along the length of the arm and the third to secure the fold where the inside back meets the inside arm. Blind buttons are more for effect than comfort and, therefore, are not deep buttons but are secured gently to create only a very slight indent in the fabric. Tie them off in the same way as those on the inside back.

step 20 Cut the fabric for the outside back and outside arms, on this chair this is one piece of fabric. Measure the outside back and outside arms and draw their outline on the fabric. Add a 6cm (2½in) allowance around the top and sides and a 10cm (4in) allowance at the bottom before cutting the fabric. Attach it to the chair frame beginning at the top, turning it under by 6cm (2½in), and temporarily securing it with small skewers. As with step 17, make small cuts in the fabric so that it lies flat around the curves. Take great care to make them the right size.

step 21 Now secure this panel of fabric with slip stitching. Begin at the base of one outside arm and work your way around to the other outside arm.

step 22 Temporary tack the fabric underneath the bottom seat rail. Make a straight cut on each side of the back legs and, carefully folding under the small section of fabric above the legs, secure the fabric on the underside of the rail. Tack the remaining top fabric to the underside of the chair. Finally, attach a dust cloth, cutting it to fit around the legs and tacking it in place around the edges.

leather club chair

This piece is one of a pair of English club chairs from around the 1920s. It is appealing because it does not have a large frame or bulky appearance but instead is more compact, with a deep seat that makes it very comfortable. Further interest is added by the gently curved back, square outline of the arms, and shaped legs. The original leather was very worn, so it was replaced with a deep chocolate-brown. New feather cushions were also added, upholstered in soft brown alcantara (faux suede). In their original coverings, club chairs are full of character; the leather has been worn in over many decades, and a rich patina has been obtained, making them hugely appealing. Initially, much of this appeal is lost with new leather, however, if good quality leather is used the chair will soon develop character again. Leather stretches over time, so it is very important to lift and pull it tightly into position, creating the right tension.

tools
Double-ended needle, magnetic hammer, scissors, staple gun (optional).

materials
Back tacking strips, cotton felt, 13mm (½in) decorative studs, dust cloth, hessian, lining cloth for seat and "flies", skin wadding, stitching thread, 13mm (½in) tacks, top fabric (including enough for "collars"), webbing.

reference
Applying a dust cloth: p83, back tacking strips: p71, making cushions: pp75–7, through stitching: p111.

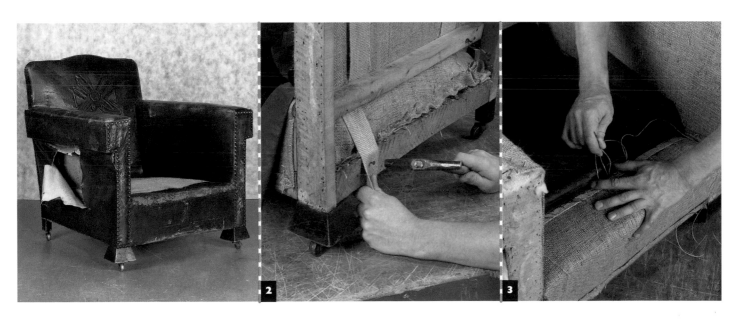

step 1 Remove the old leather and check the condition of the springs and stuffing. This chair was in good shape, requiring no serious respringing or restuffing (for details on basic techniques, see pages 40–59). The hessian on each of the arms was replaced and a small layer of stuffing was added to the seat.

step 2 Prepare the leather and lining fabric for the seat. Cut sufficient leather to reach from under the front rail, over the seat edge, and at least 20cm (8in) in from the front of the seat, meeting the lining fabric, which will continue back to under the inside back. Give both pieces an allowance of 5cm (2in). Join them using a sewing machine. Under this seam, machine sew a length of webbing. Place the cover over the seat, with the webbing left to right. Take the webbing under the bottom arm rails and attach the ends to the side rails with a tack each.

step 3 Fold the leather back over the lining. Using a double-ended needle and stitching thread, secure the strip of webbing to the seat with a line of through stitching. Take the needle down through the stuffing and webbing and out of the base of the seat, then bring it back up (see page 111). Add a layer of cotton felt on either side of the webbing, over the front of the seat and over the back of the seat.

step 4 Pull the leather over the front of the seat and secure it to the underside of the front rail with four spaced tacks. Where the leather meets the front arm upright, make a Y cut and secure it below this cut to the front of the arm facing with three spaced tacks. Make a diagonal cut in the leather above the foot of the chair, taking the leather under the front rail and across the front arm facing, and securing with tacks. Repeat this on the other arm, making a cut around each of the back uprights. Take the seat lining under the inside back rail securing it to the outside of the bottom rail with spaced tacks. On the sides, take the seat lining under each of the bottom arm rails and secure it to the outside of the side rails with spaced tacks. Once you are sure you have a good tension across the seat, gradually add more tacks to each of the rails to secure the seat cover. Trim away any excess lining and leather.

step 5 Add a layer of cotton felt over each of the arms, tucking it down between the seat and bringing it over and along the outside of the top arm rails.

step 6 Cut sufficient leather to cover the inside arm with a 10cm (4in) allowance all round. To make the most of the leather and avoid wastage, you might like to use a "fly". This is made of lining cloth or other strong remnant fabric and is simply sewn to the bottom of the leather panel where it will not be seen, that is below the level of the

seat. Turning the chair on its side, lay the leather over the arm and place three spaced tacks to the underside of the top arm rail.

step 7 Where it meets the inside back on the top arm rail, make a Y cut in the leather and make another where the base of the arm meets the inside back.

step 8 Pull the leather down under the bottom arm rail and secure it to the outside of the side rail with spaced tacks; if a fly is used this will be attached to the rail. It is very important to tension the leather really well, smoothing it down and securing it firmly to the rail. At the inside back, pull the leather around the back upright and secure it to this rail.

step 9 Where the front arm facing meets the top of the seat, fold the leather under and, pulling it across the arm facing, secure it with a tack. Continue pulling the leather around from the inside arm and place more tacks to secure it to the front arm facing. Where the top arm rail meets the back upright take the leather around this corner and secure it to the back upright with four tacks. Place more tacks on the underside of the top arm rail to secure the leather, working it to ensure good tension as you go along.

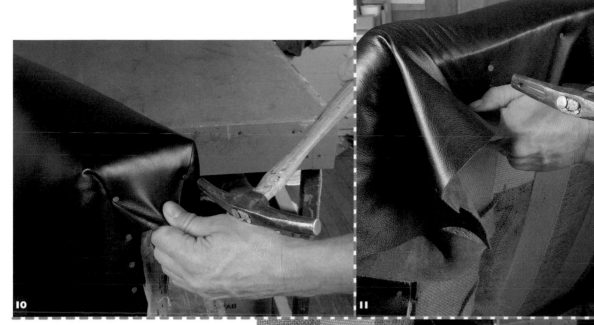

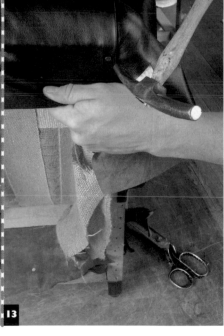

step 10 To attach the leather around the corners of the front arm facing, pull it around the top left of the arm and place a tack in the left corner of the facing about 2.5cm (1in) in, then pull the leather from around the top right of the arm and place a tack in this corner. Now pull the leather from along the top of the arm, fold it under on each side making two neat folds, and secure these with a tack on the arm facing. Repeat steps 6–10 on the other arm.

step 11 Place a layer of cotton felt over the inside back of the chair, tucking it down between the seat and the inside back and bringing it just over the head rail. Cut leather for the inside back with a 10cm (4in) allowance all round. When you cut it out, shape it around where the arms will be, leaving a 2cm (¾in) allowance. A "collar" will be needed to help the leather fit well around the top of the arms. This is a panel of top fabric used to enable fabric to fit neatly around a curve, helping avoid puckering. Place the leather over the inside back and using tailors chalk mark the curve of the arms onto the leather; cut around this shape. Now add a panel of leather around each curve, approximately 10cm (4in) deep and sew this onto the inside back, carefully around each cut-out curve. Lay the inside back panel over the chair, take it over the top of the head rail and down between the seat and inside back to the back rail. Secure it to the outside of the back rail with three spaced tacks. Now place three spaced tacks in the centre of the outside head rail, pulling

and working the leather so it is straight and tensioned. Take care to position the tacks about 3cm (1in) in from the frame as they need to be out of sight when the outside back is attached.

step 12 Make a Y cut in the leather where the inside back meets the top of the arm and a Y cut where it meets the bottom of the arm. Pull the leather through to the inside of the back upright and secure it with spaced tacks. Repeat on the other side.

step 13 Pull the leather around each of the corners at the top of the frame and secure it with a tack each time. Now pull the leather from the inside back over the head rail, make a straight, neat fold, and secure it with a tack.

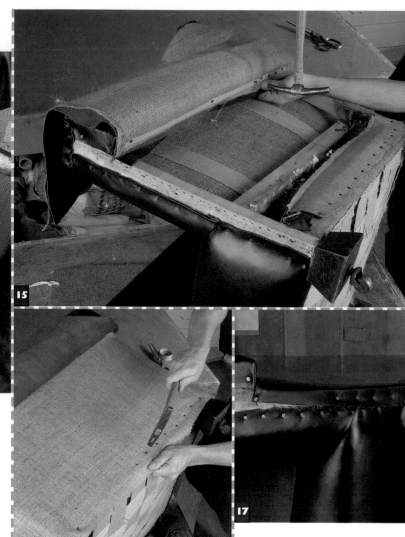

step 14 Where the inside back meets the top of the arm, take the leather around the back upright, make a neat fold, and secure it with a tack. Secure the leather at the top of the back upright with a fold and a tack. Repeat this on the opposite side. Continue to place more tacks to attach the leather to the outside back.

step 15 Cut sufficient hessian and leather for the outside arms, with a 10cm (4in) allowance all round. Turn the chair on its side, place the leather over the arm with the good side facing in and attach this with tacks to the underside of the top arm rail. Initially place spaced tacks, gradually adding more. Over this lay the hessian and attach it to the top arm rail in the same way. Next attach a length of back tacking strip with tacks. This length of purpose-made cardboard produces a clean, straight edge on a tack line. Finally add a layer of skin wadding, held in place along each of the four rails with three spaced tacks. Trim away any excess.

step 16 Pull the hessian down and, ensuring the weave is lying straight, attach it to the outside of the side rail and around onto the back upright. Trim away any excess hessian. Now pull down the leather over the hessian and attach this to the underside of the side rail with spaced tacks, working the leather and gradually adding more tacks. Take the leather around the back upright and attach it with tacks. Where the leather comes round the front upright and meets the top of the chair foot, trim it in a straight line along the bottom of the front rail and secure it to the front arm facing with a tack; at the side, fold it under, making a small cut so it will sit neatly behind the foot on the side rail and secure with a tack.

step 17 Take the rest of the leather around to the front arm facing and place a tack at the very top and down the upright, followed by further tacks to secure it. (In the picture the chair has been turned on its side to make it easier to work on the facing.)

step 18 Make a template of the front arm facing and cut this out of the leather with a 2cm (¾in) allowance all round. Lay the chair on its back, position the panel over the front arm facing and, folding it under by 2cm (¾in) place a gimp pin in the centre at the top. Work around the facing, carefully following its shape and folding the leather under to fit, ensuring it lies flat. Place tacks as you go – securing first the top, followed by the bottom and then sides – but aim to use as few as possible, one in each corner and centre ones down each sides. At the corners make a couple of small cuts to help the leather fit around and then fold it under. Repeat for the other arm.

step 19 Apply the studs over this panel. Here they are 10mm (⅜in) studs in an antique finish to complement the leather. These are secured with a small space between each. Begin at the top of the arm facing and carefully work your way down making sure the spacing is equal. Holding each stud in place, apply even pressure with the hammer to ensure the studs lie flat and straight on. Do the same to the opposite arm.

step 20 Cut out the leather for the outside back with a 2cm (¾in) allowance along the sides and the top and a 8cm (3in) allowance along the bottom. With the chair face-down on your work surface, position the leather over the outside back. Folding it under by 2cm (¾in), place a tack in the centre of each side and three spaced tacks along the top of the head rail. Work the leather as you go and make sure the folds follow the lines of the chair frame. Place spaced tacks along the underside of the back rail and trim away any excess leather.

step 21 Apply the studs in the same way as on the front arm panel (step 19), placing them approximately a little finger's-width apart. Work from the base of one side, following the frame up and around. Make a neat gently rounded fold on each of the top corners and secure the folds, initially with a tack, then a stud. Finish securing the leather to the underside of the chair with tacks.

step 22 Cut sufficient dust cloth with a 5cm (2in) allowance all round and attach this to the underside of the chair, turning it under as you attach it with tacks. The chair is now ready for the cushions (see page 77, for making box cushions).

french chairs

These late nineteenth-century French chairs have a wonderful sense of proportion and simplicity, with plain curved arms and only a small amount of detailing on the show wood. The narrow arms and sparingly stuffed back are finely balanced by the deep and generous seat. Beneath the worn white paint was the promise of natural wood – it was stripped back, revealing a wonderful plain wood, which was then hand polished to a lustrous finish. So as not to disturb the balance of the chairs' design, a plain linen was chosen for the top fabric from which a trimming of double piping was also made, emphasizing the curves on the frame. The neutral colour of the linen worked well with the newly polished wood. If you are making piping from the top fabric, be sure to order plenty of fabric for this purpose, and remember piping is best cut on the bias. Top fabric can be saved by using lining fabric for the part of the seat that will be under the cushion.

tools
Craft knife, double-ended needle, hot-glue gun, scissors, sewing machine, staple gun, web strainer.

materials
Adhesive sticks, calico, cotton felt, fibre, hessian, lining fabric, piping cord, sewing thread, skin wadding, staples, stitching twine, top fabric, webbing.

reference
Basic techniques: pp36–52, double piping: pp72–4 and p163, box cushions: p77, stitches: pp160–3, cuts, corners, and folds: pp158–9.

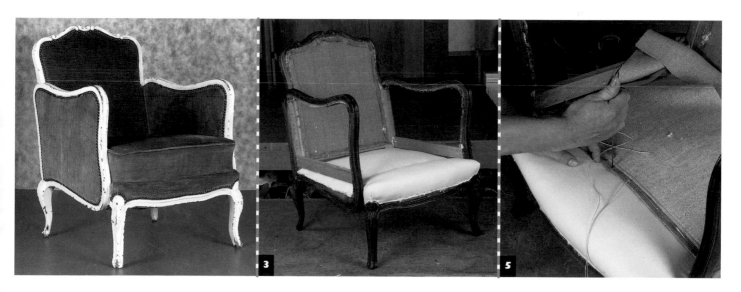

step 1 Assess the condition of the upholstery and decide what needs replacing. Here, the arms and back were stripped back; the seat was left intact with just the cotton felt and calico replaced. When there is considerable show wood, as here, it often makes more sense to use staples, rather than hammer and tacks, to avoid damaging the wood.

step 2 Staple two strips of webbing to the inside back, one top to bottom in the centre of the chair frame and the other side to side in the centre of the frame. Next add a layer of hessian, turning it over with a 2.5cm (1in) hem all round.

step 3 Apply a layer of cotton felt and calico, attaching the calico to the top of the back rail, the tops of the side rails and along the front rail. At the front, place the staples just within the frame, and not too close to the show wood; this makes it easier to trim away excess material with a craft knife. Make a series of through stitches, from behind one front upright and across to the other. After securing the twine with a slip knot on one side, take the needle down through the stuffing, out of the underside and then back up through to the top of the chair. This keeps the stuffing in place along the front edge.

step 4 Cut two panels of fabric for the seat, one out of lining fabric for the seat back (behind the row of through stitches), and one out of top fabric for the seat front, with 10cm (4in) extra all around. Machine sew the two panels together with a 1cm (½in) seam. Now machine sew along the same seam, attaching the fabric to a length of webbing enough to go from one side rail across to the other. Position the webbing and fabric over the through stitching on the seat, pull the webbing down, and staple it to both side rails.

step 5 Create another line of through stitches through the webbing to further secure and strengthen the front edge of the seat. Smooth the fabric into place on the seat.

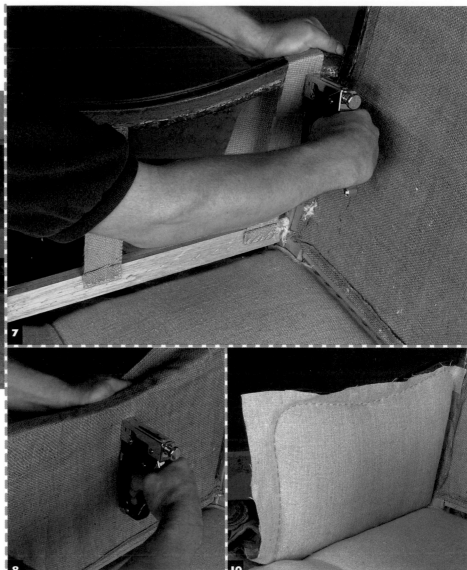

step 6 Make a T cut in towards each back upright and a Y cut around each front arm upright and pull the fabric down and around each upright. Now secure the fabric with four centre staples, one in the back rail, one in each of the side rails, and one in the front rail. Gradually place more staples, working from the centres out, leaving a small gap between each staple and space around the corners. Continually check the linen's weave is straight over the seat. Carefully fold the fabric around each front corner. Trim away the excess fabric from around all the rails of the chair seat.

step 7 Next, work on the arms. Attach two strips of webbing vertically to the inside arm panels, one close to the inside back and one just off-centre. Take care when working close to the show wood.

step 8 Cut a piece of hessian with a 5cm (2in) allowance all round and attach this to the inside arm with the staple gun. Place centre staples in the top of the frame, the bottom arm rail, and halfway up the front upright. Where the back of the arm meets the inside back, take the hessian inbetween the webbing and the back upright, but leave it unattached. On the top, bottom, and front edges, turn the hessian over with a 2.5cm (1in) hem and attach it with more staples. Trim away the excess around the edges.

step 9 Add two layers of cotton felt over the hessian, smoothing them down so they lie just inside the line of the frame. Make the inner layer slightly smaller than the outer one to create a good shape. Add a layer of calico, cutting it with a 5cm (2in) allowance all round. Initially place centre staples in the same way as the hessian (step 8) but only in the top and front of the chair arm, ensuring the weave is straight. Pull the calico down and under the arm rail, leaving this side unattached. Pull it through where it meets the inside back, again leaving it unattached. Place more staples on the top and front of the arm frame, working from the centre out.

step 10 Attach the top fabric to the inside arm. Cut sufficient fabric and allow an extra 5cm (2in) all round. Secure this in the same way as the calico, initially with two centre staples, gradually adding more. Take the fabric down under the arm frame and attach it to the bottom rail. The calico can now be secured with staples in the same way. Take the fabric through the frame at the back of the arm, but leave it unattached. As you apply the staples, continually check the weave of the linen is lying straight and be careful not to mark the show wood. Trim away the excess fabric. Repeat the same process on the other arm.

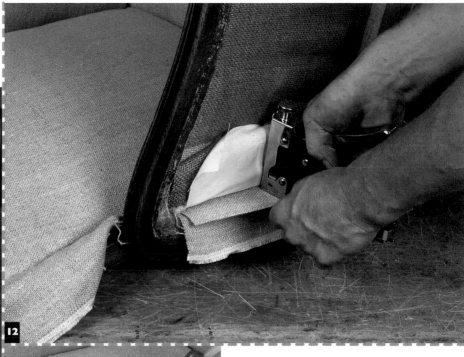

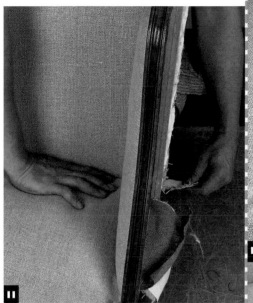

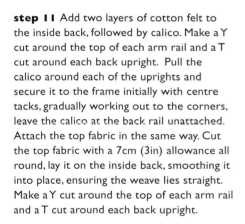

step 11 Add two layers of cotton felt to the inside back, followed by calico. Make a Y cut around the top of each arm rail and a T cut around each back upright. Pull the calico around each of the uprights and secure it to the frame initially with centre tacks, gradually working out to the corners, leave the calico at the back rail unattached. Attach the top fabric in the same way. Cut the top fabric with a 7cm (3in) allowance all round, lay it on the inside back, smoothing it into place, ensuring the weave lies straight. Make a Y cut around the top of each arm rail and a T cut around each back upright.

step 12 Pull the fabric through between the inside arm frame and the inside back, and attach it with staples to the inside rim of the arm frame. Pull the fabric down between the inside back and the seat and staple it to the back rail. Trim away all the excess fabric along the line of the show wood. The fabric and calico of the inside arm can now be secured in place with staples on the frame where the arm meets the inside back.

step 13 Work on the outside arms. Attach a piece of hessian with staples, turning over a 2.5cm (1in) hem. Over this, lay some skin wadding and hold it in place with a centre staple on the frame top, and one in each of the top corners. Next attach the top fabric,

initially with centre staples, then gradually working around adding more staples. Trim away the excess fabric.

step 14 Prepare the double piping. Measure sufficient piping cord to go all around the inside and outside of the arms, the inside and outside back and along the front edge of the seat, adding an allowance of 10cm (4in) for each section, then double this length. Make the piping (see pages 74 and 163).

step 15 Attach the piping to the inside arm panel where it meets the top of the seat. Using the glue gun, carefully run the adhesive over the staples around the inside arm and lay the piping over the top, applying pressure as you go along. Continue up and around the inside back of the chair and down to the other side and along the arm. Attach piping along the front edge of the seat in the same way.

step 16 Prepare the outside back. Attach a layer of hessian in the same way as the outside arms (step 13), again turning it over with 2.5cm (1in) hem. Next, add a layer of skin wadding and trim away any excess. Add the top fabric with four centre staples, one on the top, one on each side, and one on the bottom rail. Following the curves of the frame, trim away the excess fabric. Attach the double piping. As the piping join will be visible on the outside arms and the outside back, begin attaching it at the bottom centre, which is the least conspicuous place. Apply adhesive to a small section at one end of the piping, press this against the frame and turn the rest of the piping over, creating a neat fold. Apply pressure and temporarily hold it in position with a small pin. Continue attaching the piping and when you reach the starting place again, make a fold in the piping and butt the end up to the first fold in a tight, clean line. Attach the piping to the outside arms in the same way.

step 17 Make the cover for the seat cushion. The seams for the cushions on this chair were sewn with saddle stitch but piping could also be used. (see page 77 for making a box seat cusion).

wing chair

This early twentieth-century wing chair is quite special because it is so plain in design, with no bulky stuffing or fancy turned arms. Its slim back, wings, and arms give it a very clean and well-defined appearance. In order to accentuate these simple lines, a striped fabric was chosen to re-cover it. Because there is so little on the chair to interfere with it, this bold design, with its cream base and luxurious black velvet stripe, works very well. A subtle trimming of single piping in black velvet further enhances the sleek lines of the chair, which is for light domestic use only. A wing chair takes a little more time to reupholster than an ordinary one as the two wings create additional work and careful consideration needs to be given to the order in which the re-covering is done. This chair was in poor condition and needed stripping right back to the wood. Before reupholstering work began, the back and front legs were polished.

tools
Circular needle, craft knife, magnetic hammer, regulator, staple gun (optional), scissors, web strainer.

materials
Back tacking strips, barrier cloth, cotton felt, fibre, gimp pins, hessian, skin wadding, stitching twine, 13mm (½in) tacks, top fabric, webbing.

reference
Basic techniques: pp36–59, applying a dust cloth: p83, cuts, corners, and folds: pp158–9, stitches: pp160–3 (bridle ties: p162).

step 1 Remove the outer layers along with all of the old stuffing, leaving the chair as a bare carcase. On the underside of the seat, attach five webs from front to back and four webs from side to side. Add two webs to each of the inside arms and three to the inside back; secure them vertically with tacks and space them evenly along the rails.

step 2 Cut hessian for the inside back and arms, allowing an extra 5cm (2in) all round. On one inside arm, secure the hessian, turning it over with a 2cm (¾in) hem and apply a centre tack to the bottom arm rail and one to the top arm rail. Continue with spaced tacks, working from the centre out. Repeat this on the other inside arm and on the inside back.

step 3 Attach two strips of webbing to each wing along the top of the head rail, leaving the bottom ends of the webbing free. Secure a layer of hessian, with a 2cm (¾in) turned-over hem, to the inside wing, placing spaced tacks along the top of the head rail and the wing upright. Leave the hessian unattached along the bottom wing rail and the back upright.

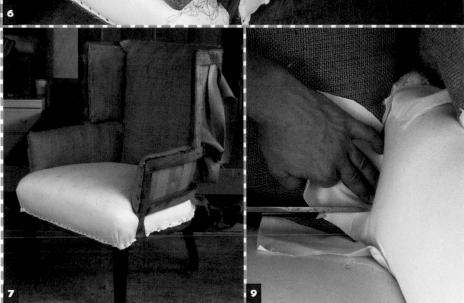

step 4 Spring and stuff the seat, and add a layer of calico (see pages 53–9).

step 5 Stitch a series of bridle ties, with which to hold the fibre, on the inside arms and inside back. Make two rows of two large loops on the inside arms and three rows of two large loops on the inside back. Add a good quantity of fibre under these loops. As you pull in the ties, adjust the fibre to ensure there are no lumps or dips and that it is evenly placed.

step 6 Apply a layer of hessian, with an allowance of 10cm (4in) all round, to further secure the fibre on the inside arms. Place three spaced tacks along the top of the top arm rail. Make Y cuts around the wing upright and the back upright at the top of the arm and around the bottom of the back upright and around the front upright. Take the hessian under the bottom arm rail and secure it with tacks to the outside edge of this rail, then take the hessian around the back upright but leave unattached. Continue to place further tacks along the top of the arm and down the front upright, ensuring the weave is lying straight and using the regulator to even out the stuffing underneath. Repeat this process on the other arm.

step 7 Apply hessian to the inside back in the same way. Tuck it under the inside back rail and attach it to the outside edge of the rail and then to the top of the head rail. Pull it around the back uprights, making Y cuts to fit it around the arm rails, and secure it to the side edge of each upright.

step 8 Cut some cotton felt for the inside arms. Lay it over the arms, carefully tucking it down where it meets the seat. It should be flush with the front edge of the arm and run just along the top of the arm frame. Where it meets the chair back, cut it to fit. When the calico is fitted (step 9), it will pull the cotton felt just around the front edge of the arm and just over the top edge.

step 9 Cut sufficient calico for the inside arms with a 12cm (4¾in) allowance all round. On each arm, place three centre tacks to secure it: one over the top of the top arm rail, one on the the bottom arm rail, and one around the front edge of the arm upright. Make Y cuts in to the back and wing uprights and in to the front of the arm. Take the calico through and around to the outside back but do not attach it. Continue to place tacks, working from the centre out towards the edges. Ensure you are creating sufficient tension across the calico to produce a good shape on the inside arm. On the front top of the arm, around the corner, fold and tuck the calico under and secure it with a tack.

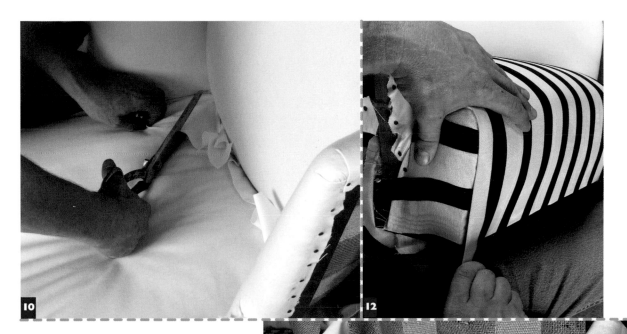

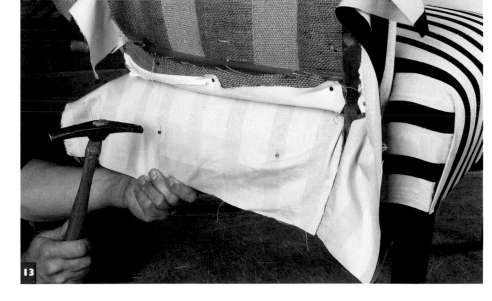

step 10 Apply calico to the inside back, tacking it to the outside of the head rail. Make a T cut around the back uprights and a Y cut around the top arm rails. Pull the calico through and around the back uprights, attaching it to their outside edges and then pull it down under the inside back rail securing it to the bottom back rail. Secure it at the top by taking it over the head rail, on to the outside edge.

step 11 Cut the top fabric for the seat adding an extra 15cm (6in) all round. With striped fabric, it is very important to ensure that the stripes always lie straight, and that when the different parts of the chair come together (such as where the inside back meets the top of the seat) the stripes will line up exactly. Smooth the fabric across the seat. Cut around the front arm uprights and around the back uprights, and tuck the fabric down between the seat and the inside back and between the seat and the inside arms. Now place a centre tack on the outside of the back rail and on the outside of the side rails; around the front, place a tack on the underside of the front rail. Ensuring the line of the fabric is still straight, continue to place spaced tacks around the frame, leaving 5cm (2in) around the corners.

step 12 To work the fabric around the front corners of the seat, pull it down the side edge, in front of the arm, and secure it with a tack under the side rail. Fold the fabric around the front edge of the seat, cut away the excess, and pull the fabric down from the top of the seat, folding it under itself to create a sharp fold along the vertical edge of the corner. Secure this fold at the bottom with a temporary tack. Make a straight cut to the inside of each front leg; take the fabric underneath the seat and secure it with a tack. Around the side and front edge of each leg, tuck the fabric under, replacing the temporary tack with a gimp pin. Now secure all the fabric along the underneath of all the seat rails.

step 13 Cut the fabric for the inside arms, making sure the pattern matches on both arms and adding a 15cm (6in) allowance all round. Make a Y cut around the front arm upright and around the wing upright and two T cuts around the back upright. Pull the fabric around each of the uprights and down underneath the bottom arm rail. Place spaced tacks along the side rail and down the front arm upright and along the top arm rail, leave the fabric around the back upright unattached.

step 14 Where the top arm rail meets the top of the front arm upright pull the fabric around the upright and secure at the top with a tack. Now take the fabric from the inside of the rail over the top to lie over the fabric you have just secured and make a neat fold by tucking it under itself, so the folded edge sits on the top of the corner. Secure this with a tack on the outside of the rail. When you are happy that the fabric is lying as it should, add the remaining tacks to the top arm rail, down the front arm upright and along the side rail, and trim away the excess fabric. Repeat steps 13 and 14 to cover the other inside arm.

step 15 Cut sufficient fabric to cover the inside back and include an extra 15cm (6in) all round. Spread the fabric over the chair back, taking time to line up the stripes with those on the seat. Secure the fabric at the top with three tacks on the outside of the head rail. At the bottom, tuck it down between the inside back and the seat.

step 16 On the back rail make several cuts in the top fabric to help it sit well around the curve. Secure the fabric to the rail with spaced tacks.

step 17 Where the back uprights meet the top arm rails and the headrail make Y cuts in the fabric and a T cut around the base of each back upright. Pull the fabric around the uprights and secure with spaced tacks. Continue securing the fabric, placing further tacks to the headrail, back rail, and uprights.

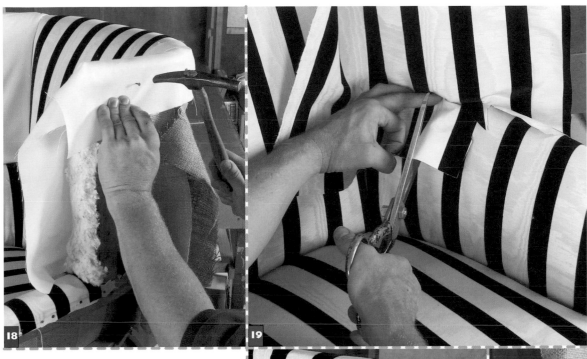

step 18 Add cotton felt to each wing, cutting enough to allow it to come around the wing upright. Cut sufficient calico, including a 10cm (4in) allowance all round. Position the calico around the wing frame and place spaced tacks on the outside of the frame along the top and the wing upright, folding it neatly round the front corner. Leave the bottom edge and where the fabric meets the back upright unattached. Be sure to create a smooth and well shaped pad on which to apply the top fabric. Repeat the process on the other wing.

step 19 Cut top fabric to cover the inside wings with an extra 10cm (4in) all round. Place the fabric over the inside wing frame and carefully line it up with the pattern of the inside arm. At the top, attach it to the outside of the head rail with three temporary tacks. Make a Y cut in to the wing upright and take the fabric over the top of the arm and around the wing upright. Take it between the bottom of the wing and the top arm rail, and attach it with three temporary tacks to the outside of the top arm rail.

step 20 Hammer home the temporary tacks. Make cuts around the back upright where it meets the wing at the top and the botom, take the fabric through the frame, and attach it to the back upright. Pull the fabric around the front of the wing upright and, folding it neatly on the front corner, secure it to the outside of the wing upright. Continually check the pattern is lying as it should and the fabric is taut across the frame. Repeat steps 19 and 20 on the other wing, ensuring the pattern matches.

step 21 Attach the remaining calico, followed by the hessian, on to the outside of both wing frames in the same way as the top fabric, trimming away any excess. Finally, secure the lower ends of the wing webbing to the top edge of the arm rails.

step 22 Trim away excess calico, hessian, and top fabric from around the chair. Attach the single piping to the frame, beginning at the base of one arm. Secure one end of the piping to the outside edge of the front arm rail, where it meets the seat fabric, leaving an end of 5cm (2in), which is attached to the underside of the frame later. Attaching the piping with spaced tacks and taking care that it lies straight, work up the arm rail. Create a neat corner at the top of the rail by placing one tack at the highest vertical point, changing direction to take the piping horizontally along the arm, and placing another tack on this side of the corner. Continue attaching the piping until it reaches the wing upright and secure it here, leaving a loose end. Do the same on the other arm.

step 23 Take another length of piping and secure it to the bottom outside edge of the wing upright meeting the piping already in place. Continue up the wing, creating a corner where it meets the top rail, along the top of the back frame, and down the opposite wing upright. Secure the piping at the bottom of the upright, where it meets the top arm rail, again leaving a good margin.

step 24 Prepare the outside wings for the top fabric. Cut the hessian with a 5cm (2in) allowance all round and attach it to the outside wing frame with spaced tacks, folding it over with a 2.5cm (1in) hem along the top and down the sides of the frame. Trim away any excess hessian and then secure it at the bottom to the top arm rail (this does not need to be hemmed).

step 25 Cut top fabric for the outside wing with a 10cm (4in) allowance. Align the top edge just below the piping and then turn it over so the good side lies against the inside wing (if you are using a patterned fabric, take time to align it exactly). Place a length of back tacking strip over the reverse side of the fabric at the top of the frame and attach it with spaced tacks so it lies snugly beneath the line of piping, creating a clean line along the top of the frame. Bring the fabric down over the outside wing and smooth it into place. Place spaced tacks along the bottom edge of the fabric where it meets the top arm rail and along the back upright. Carefully pin the fabric in place down the length of the front wing upright, folding it under, and then slip stitch it just inside the line of the piping. Repeat the process on the other outside wing.

step 26 Cut a length of hessian to fit around the outside back arm with a 5cm (2in) allowance all round. Attach this to the outside arm frame with spaced tacks, folding over a 2.5cm (1in) margin along the top of the rail and down the side of the front upright. Trim away any excess.

step 27 Attach the fabric to the outside arm in the same way as on the outside wing: align the top edge of the fabric just under the piping, turn it over so that the good side is lying over the inside arm, and, using a back tacking strip, secure it with spaced tacks to the top of the outside rail. This creates a clean line just below the length of piping.

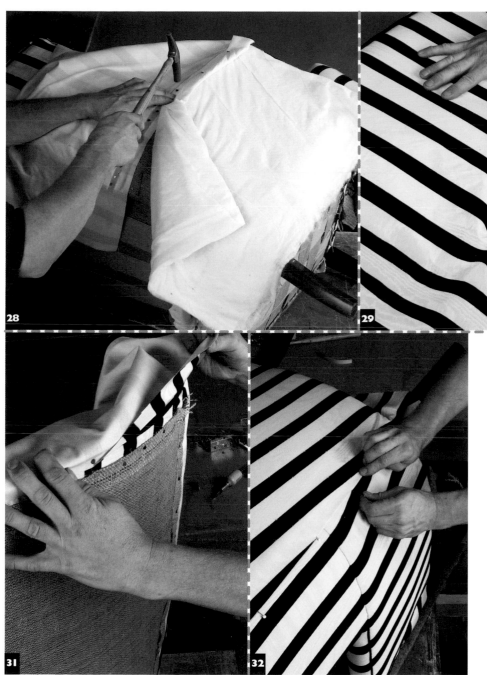

step 30 Repeat this process on the outside back, applying a layer of hessian, followed by a layer of skin wadding. Fold the hessian over along the top rail and down the sides, but at the bottom attach it without a hem. As before, position the top fabric with the good side facing the inside back and match the pattern at the top.

step 31 Attach the fabric with spaced tacks along the top rail and then secure a length of back tacking strip with tacks along the top just below the line of piping.

step 32 Taking the fabric over the back tacking strip, smooth it down, ensure the weave lies straight, and attach it to the underside of the chair frame. Secure each side with pins, creating a neat fold down the length of each back upright, and then, taking your time, slip stitch each of these seams. Tack the bottom edge off underneath the seat rail.

step 33 Finish the chair by attaching a dust cloth, cutting around the legs (see page 83).

step 28 Add a layer of skin wadding on to the outside arm, folding it over with a 2.5cm (1in) margin along the top of the arm rail. Attach this with spaced tacks along the top and sides of the arm frame and then, smoothing it down, trim it along the bottom just below the side rail.

step 29 Folding the top fabric back over the wadding, smooth it down the length of the outside arm, then attach it to the underside of the frame. Make a straight cut in the fabric around the top of the back leg. Where the arm meets the front upright, join it to the inside arm fabric with a slip stitch seam. Finally, secure the fabric with tacks down the length of the back upright. Repeat steps 28 and 29 on the other arm.

g plan chair

G Plan chairs were designed in the 1960s and sold widely during the 1960s and 1970s. They are very distinctive and wonderfully comfortable with the added attraction that they rock as well as swivel. This original G Plan chair was still in its orginal cover – a rather grubby golden velour. To give it a more contemporary look, a soft leather in a warm neutral tone has been chosen to reupholster it (an alternative fabric of similar tone would work equally well). As it is effectively a wing chair, it is quite a complicated and lengthy undertaking, so plenty of time needs to be put aside to tackle it. The materials used to make the chair are still relatively modern, which means that it is appropriate to use modern tools and materials during the reupholstering process, including staples, ply grip, and foam. With an item of this age, it is highly advisable to replace materials, such as the foam, with the latest versions that conform to modern fire regulations.

tools
Bread/carving knife, craft knife, hammer, metal cutters (similar to pliers), scissors, screwdriver, sewing machine, staple gun, tape measure, wooden rule.

materials
Back tacking strips, dust cloth, 10cm (4in) foam, lining fabric, piping cord, ply grip, polyester wadding, staples, tailor's chalk, top fabric.

reference
Deep buttoning: pp60–3 and pp101–2, single piping: p74 and p163, box cushions: p77, applying a dust cloth: p83.

This G Plan chair has been constructed using more modern upholstery materials. These include Pirelli webbing – a rubber webbing that can be used to form a strong base on which to hold a seat cushion; foam, which is used to stuff the seat cushion and also form the padding on the inside back; serpentine (zig zag) springs, which have been used to support the back of the chair; and ply grip, which is used here to firmly secure the leather to the frame.

step 1 Remove the cushion but do not discard as it will be useful to refer to when making up a new cushion. Detach the chrome and wooden base from the chair and then carefully remove all the old top fabric and any old and worn layers of materials such as wadding or cotton felt. If required, replace the foam with one that meets safety standards. Add a new layer of wadding over each of the arms.

step 2 Begin by making a sleeve for the front part of the seat. The sleeve will encompass the entire front section of the seat; the remainder of the seat, made up from ruberized webbing, will be covered with lining cloth at a later stage (step17). Cut out a panel of leather to the width of the front rail and allow enough length for it to go under the rail and around to its back. Place it over the front of the chair to check the fit. Make the rest of the cover by cutting two side panels and sewing the pieces together on the sewing machine.

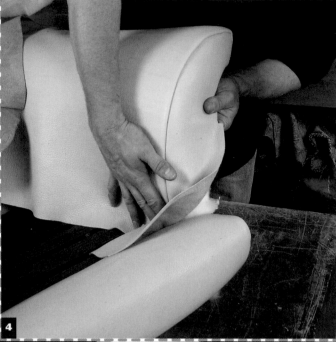

step 3 To make best use of materials, you may wish to attach a fly to the leather where it will be under the seat (see page 106, step 6, for more information on flys); simply sew this piece of lining material on to the back edge of the panel of leather. Fit the sleeve over the front rail, cutting around each of the front arm uprights. Attach the sleeve under the front of the chair with spaced staples. Wrap the opposite end of the sleeve around the back of the rail and under it, attaching it to the underside with spaced staples (in the picture it is the fly that is being stapled) . Work the leather, pulling it taut, as you go. Place staples around the side panels where they meet the base of the front arm uprights; site them as close to the base of the uprights as possible so the inside arm leather will cover them at a later stage.

step 4 Make a sleeve for the inside arm, and arm facing in the same way (making a template for the front arm facing before cutting the leather). Cut each piece of leather with a 10cm (4in) allowance and make the piece for the front arm facing long enough to reach the base of the front arm upright. Sew the two pieces together and then fit the sleeve over the arm.

step 5 Where the inside arm meets the front of the seat make a small diagonal cut in the leather to allow it to fit around the front of the seat, and pull it down, creating a taut fit. Secure it to the underside of the side rail with staples.

step 6 Apply four spaced staples to the outside of the top arm rail and down the outside of the front arm upright. Make a series of cuts where the leather fits around the inside of the curve to allow it to sit neatly. The leather cannot be taken under the bottom arm rail because of the rubber strips that form the seat, so staple it to the inside edge of the bottom arm rail.

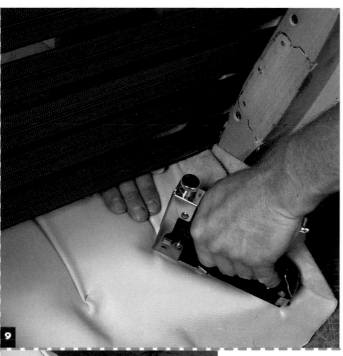

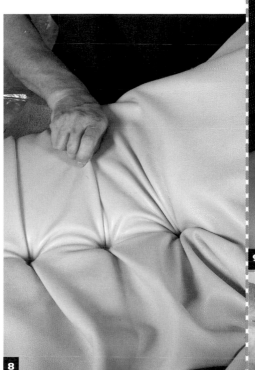

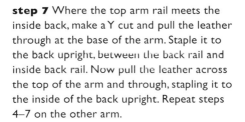

step 7 Where the top arm rail meets the inside back, make a Y cut and pull the leather through at the base of the arm. Staple it to the back upright, between the back rail and inside back rail. Now pull the leather across the top of the arm and through, stapling it to the inside of the back upright. Repeat steps 4–7 on the other arm.

step 8 Place a layer of polyester wadding over the foam on the inside back and secure it to the frame with spaced staples. Then prepare the leather for the inside back. See pages 60–3 and 98–103 for guidance on measuring for the inside back fabric on a chair with buttons and the process of applying the fabric and attaching the buttons to the chair back. When attaching the leather to the top of the chair back take care to create neat, straight folds in the leather as it goes over the head rail, securing the folds on the back with staples.

step 9 When all the buttons have been attached to the chair, make Y cuts in the leather where the inside back meets the base of the arms. Pull the leather under the inside back rail, down towards the back rail, and again, creating neat, straight folds in the leather, secure it with a series of staples to the back rail. Make sure the base of each fold is held firmly in place with staples. Make Y cuts in the leather where it meets the top of each arm and pull it through and around the sides of each back upright. Secure with staples.

step 10 Prepare the piping for the outside arms and the outside back. Either make piping using the same leather or buy it ready-made in leather or a different fabric. Have the lengths of piping as long as possible, so there will be fewer joins. Trim away any excess leather around the outside arm and outside back. Beginning with the outside arm, staple the piping to the underside of the side rail, where it meets the front upright. Now staple the piping around the outside arm, up the edges of the wing panels, along the top of head rail and down the other wing panel and then along the other arm. Go slowly and carefully follow the contours of the frame. On reaching the bottom of the arm, take the piping under the side rail and secure it here with more staples. Trim away any excess piping under the base.

step 11 Cut sufficient leather for each of the outside arms with a 10cm (4in) allowance all round. Turn the chair on its side and position the leather so it rests over the top of the arm with the good side facing down. Place a series of staples to attach the leather to the underside of the top arm rail, placing the staples to fit snugly just below the length of piping. Now take a length of back tacking strip and secure this with staples along the same line on the top arm rail. The back tacking strip will achieve a clean, straight line along this staple line. Now add a layer of polyester wadding over the outside arm and hold it in place with four centre staples.

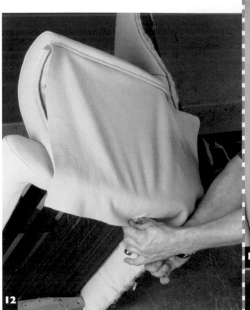

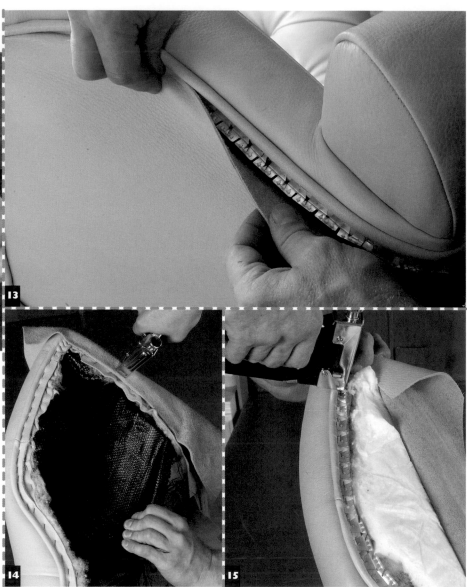

step 12 Pull the leather down the length of the outside arm, and, having creating a good taut finish, secure it to the underside of the side rail.

step 13 Use a strip of ply grip to attach the leather around the corner of the outside arm and down the length of the front arm facing. The ply grip allows the leather to be attached securely without the need for blind stitching. It works by gripping the leather with metal teeth, which can then be folded and hammered down to create a neat finish. Ply grip is typically used on more modern pieces of furniture. If you are using it for the first time, practise first, taking care not to cut yourself on the sharp metal teeth. Using metal cutters, cut a sufficient length of ply grip to run around the curve of the arm and down the side. Attach the side that has perforated holes in it to the chair using the staple gun. Trim the leather around the curve and down the front arm upright leaving a 1cm (⅜in) allowance and then turn it over the ply grip so it sits over the metal teeth. Hammer the leather down so the ply grip bites into it, holding it in place. Work your way down to the side rail. Cut away any excess ply grip and pull the leather under the side rail. Secure it to the underside with staples. Carry out the same process on the other arm.

step 14 Cut out the leather for the outside of the wing frames with a 10cm (4in) allowance all round. Folding the leather over the back of the chair so the good side is facing down, secure it along the head rail, just below the line of piping using the staple gun. Now attach a line of back tacking strip in the same way as the arms.

step 15 Before folding the leather back over the head rail, attach a layer of polyester wadding using staples. Now take the leather back over the head rail and secure it to the back upright with a series of staples. Next, in the same way as the outside arm, attach a strip of ply grip down the length of the outside wing. Trim away the leather leaving a 1cm (⅜in) allowance. Making a neat fold where the head rail meets the top of the wing upright, begin to fold the leather over the ply grip, then push it down to secure it. Ensure it is attached right beside the length of piping. At the bottom of the wing upright, attach a small piece of ply grip where it meets the top of the outside arm and, trimming the leather sufficiently to allow it to be folded under, secure it to the ply grip.

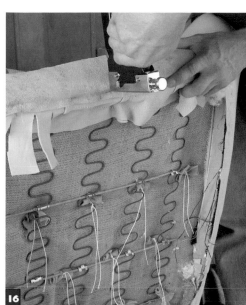

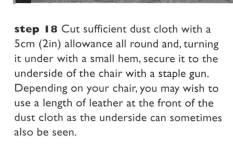

step 16 Cut sufficient leather for the outside back with a 10cm (4in) allowance all round. Secure the leather across the head rail and add a back tacking strip in the same way as the outside wing and outside arm (steps 11 and 14). Now attach a layer of wadding using staples. Attach a length of ply grip down each back upright. Fold the leather back over the head rail and trim away any excess down each side, leaving a 1cm (³⁄₈in) allowance. Making a neat fold in each of the top corners, fold the leather over the ply grip and secure it as before. Secure the leather to the underside of the back rail with staples and trim away any excess.

step 17 Attach the lining. On this chair the lining is decorative, serving only to cover the rubber strips that form the base of the seat. Cut sufficient lining fabric with a 10cm (4in) allowance at the front and back and a 3cm (1in) allowance along each side. On the sewing machine make a neat hem along each of the sides, turning the fabric under by 3cm (1in). Place this panel of fabric over the seat, taking the front end over the last strip of rubber and attaching it to the back of the front rail using the staple gun. Do the same at the back, taking it over the last rubber strip and attaching it to the underside of the back rail. The sides of the lining are not attached because there is too much movement in the rubber strips when the chair is sat on.

step 18 Cut sufficient dust cloth with a 5cm (2in) allowance all round and, turning it under with a small hem, secure it to the underside of the chair with a staple gun. Depending on your chair, you may wish to use a length of leather at the front of the dust cloth as the underside can sometimes also be seen.

step 19 Make a template for the seat cushion and using a wooden rule, measure out the shape on the 10cm (4in) foam. Referring to the old cushion here will be helpful. The foam shape can be cut either using a sharp bread knife or an electric carving knife. Make a box cushion cover for the foam (see page 77).

box stool

This late nineteenth-century box stool has a wonderful shape with dainty carved feet. To accentuate and enhance the voluptuous curves of the piece, a sumptuous red suede, with a soft tactile texture, was used to re-cover it, the inside was lined with opulent silk and satin, and a single line of ruby red velvet piping was added along the line of each curve. A couple of velvet flowers provide the final detail. This is a relatively straightforward project, but the curved sides need a little attention to ensure a good fit. Like leather, suede will give considerably and, therefore, needs to be stretched across the frame to fit well. Staples are preferable to tacks with this type of piece, as they lie flatter against the surface. They are also more suitable for suede, which is vulnerable to damage. When working with suede be sure to use a clean work bench, preferably covered with something soft; we used an old board covered in a thick fabric, which made it easy to turn the box around and kept the suede protected.

tools
Circular slipping needle, craft knife, hot-glue gun, marker pen, pins, scissors, sewing machine, small skewers, staple gun, tailor's chalk.

Materials
Adhesive sticks, back tacking strips, calico, velvet ribbon, dust cloth, fibre, hessian, single velvet piping, plywood, skin wadding, template fabric, thread, top fabric.

Reference
Top stuffing: pp45–7, over stuffing: pp48–52, piping: pp72–4, applying a dust cloth: p83, wall stitch: p160.

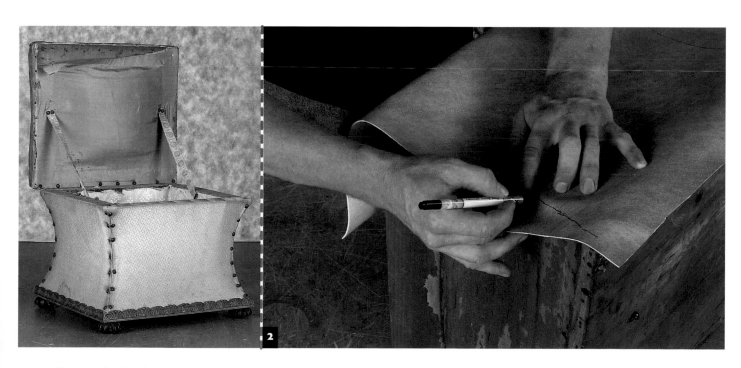

step 1 Remove the feet from the box and unscrew the bracket hinges that attach the lid to the box, keeping them for reference or reuse if they are in reasonable condition. Strip off the old covering, removing all the old tacks. Discard the stuffing on the lid.

step 2 The covering on the outside of this box is made up of four separate panels. Three seams are sewn on the sewing machine, the fourth is sewn by hand on the box. In order to achieve the desired end results, the suede needs to fit like a glove so it is very important to get the pattern exactly right. Lay a piece of calico, or something similar, over each of the panels and draw their outline with a marker pen. There may be small differences between the panels so it's a good idea to make individual patterns for each one. Lay the suede out flat, transfer the pattern shapes on to it using tailor's chalk, and then cut out each panel with a 2.5cm (1in) allowance all around. When positioning the pattern on the suede, check there are no marks on the visible side.

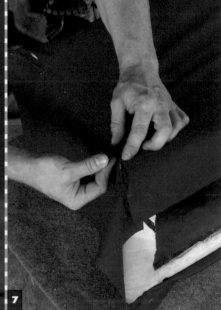

step 3 Cut the skin wadding to size with a small allowance along the bottom edge and a little extra on the top to take it over the rims, which will soften the wooden edges. Attach the wadding to each panel with two spaced staples down each side.

step 4 On the piece of suede that will make up the back panel, pin a length of piping along one of the side edges, following the marking for the seam made with the marker pen (or tailor's chalk) as in step 2. Machine sew the piping in place, just to the points where the suede will eventually turn on to the top rim and the base of the box. You may need a special needle for stitching suede on your sewing machine as materials like suede and leather are quite tough and so need a strong needle – check with an upholstery supplier to see if your current sewing machine needles are sufficient. Pin and then machine sew one of the side panels to the other edge of the back panel, incorporating piping and making sure that the seam follows the chalk markings. Now sew one edge of the front panel to this side panel, again incorporating piping, and then the remaining side panel to the other edge of the front panel, along with a length of piping. Before sewing, make sure the suede is facing the right way and the correct edges are joined. Make small, spaced cuts in the allowance along each seam so the panels will sit more easily along the curved edges of the box; take care not to cut too close to the stitches.

step 5 Staple the open edge of the back panel along the corresponding curved back edge of the box, but not over on to either the top rim or the base. Ensure that the piping follows the curve exactly. Take the side panel of suede around the side of box, smoothing it in place so the lines of piping sit precisely along each of the curved edges, easing it along the way.

step 6 Smooth the final panel of suede onto the side panel of the box so that it butts along the curved edge with the back panel. Temporarily pin these two panels of suede together at the top and bottom of the box. Flatten out the seam allowance and make small cuts in the suede so it will sit more easily on the curve.

step 7 Turn under the allowance and hold the seam in place with small skewers, leaving the suede at the top and bottom rims free.

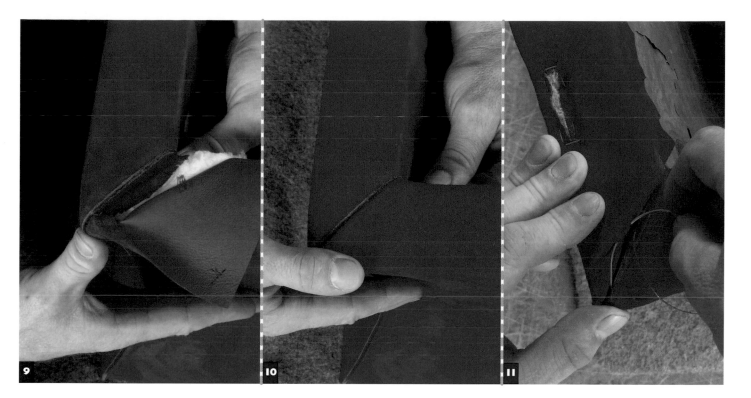

step 8 Smooth the suede over the top rim of the box and down into the inside. Staple it along the top of the inside panels, stopping 5cm (2in) away from each of the corners. Place spaced staples initially, adding more once you are happy with the way the suede fits around the box.

step 9 On one side of one top corner, pull the suede and piping taut across the rim, from the outside to the inside of the box. Holding the suede and the piping securely, staple them in place inside the box. Trim away the excess suede.

step 10 On the other side of the corner fold the suede under so it lies neatly alongside the piping, effectively mitring the two panels. Secure the suede on the inside of the box with a staple. Repeat steps 9 and 10 on the other three top corners. Mitre the bottom corners, stapling them in place on the underside of the box.

step 11 Using a circular slipping needle and matching thread, slip stitch together the mitres around each of the top corners. On the fourth side, currently held together with skewers, slip stitch all the way down the side edge. Along the back rim of the box, locate where the hinges sit using your fingers. Carefully cut out some fabric here to reveal where the screws will go, leaving a small allowance inside the circumference, and staple around the hole you have made. The aim is to enable the hinges to sit snugly, lying flush with the top fabric, so keep this as neat as possible.

step 12 Make a pattern for the inside panels in the same way as for the outside panels (step 2). Cut the lining fabric to the pattern shape leaving a 2.5cm (1in) hem allowance all around. Use the sewing machine to attach all four seams, again sewing along the chalk markings, so creating a tube. Leave the top and bottom open.

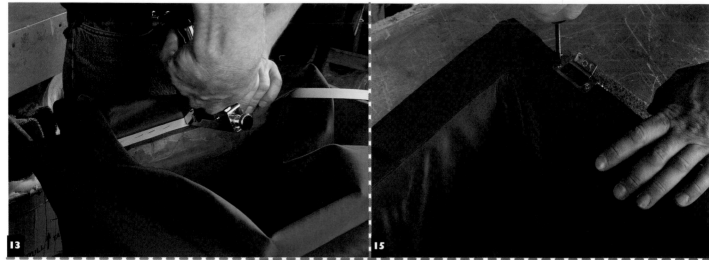

step 13 Staple two lengths of double-sided velvet ribbon to the inside edge of the box at the centre point of each side panel which will hold the box lid in place (see step 21). Turn the tube of lining fabric right-side out. Place it upside down on the top of the box so that one side panel of lining faces the corresponding box panel and the top edge of the lining sits 2.5cm (1in) below the top edge of the box. Position a back tacking strip on the lining so that it is level with the rim of the box and staple it in place (as it is in the picture), first at each end and then along its length making sure it continues to lie absolutely straight. Repeat this along the remaining three panels.

step 14 Pull the lining fabric down through the box, smoothing it down the sides and keeping it taut, and staple it to the bottom of the box. Initially use a centre staple on each side and then work your way to each corner leaving a space of 2.5cm (1in) around each corner. Carefully fold the fabric under at each corner and staple.

step 15 Re-attach the hinges to the top of the box, making sure they lie straight along the back edge.

step 16 Making a pattern first, cut a piece of plywood to the shape of the inside base of the box. Staple a layer of skin wadding to this. Cut a piece of fabric to cover the wadding, allowing for a hem of 5cm (2in) all round. Turn this over and secure the fabric on the underside of the plywood with staples: apply a centre staple on each side and then work out to the corners. At the corners, fold the excess fabric under itself and, holding the fabric down, staple around the corners. Drop the base into the box.

step 17 Staple a layer of hessian over the webbing on the top side of the lid, turning it over with a 1.5cm (½in) hem. On top of this, add a good amount of fibre, teasing it out and taking it to the edges of the lid. Attach another layer of hessian, turning under the hem, to create a pad. Sew a row of wall stitch around each edge of the pad. Add a layer of cotton felt and then a layer of calico, making sure you make a smooth, elegant shape over the lid. Place a centre staple on each edge of the underside of the lid to secure the calico, gradually adding more, and folding around and securing the corners last.

step 18 Cut a piece of suede with a 6cm (2½in) allowance all round and attach this in the same way as the calico. Make a simple fold around each of the corners. Place the staples at least 2cm (¾in) away from the edge of the lid so they do not get in the way when the lining for the lid is attached.

step 19 Attach a piece of calico to the underside of the lid, turning it over with a small hem and attaching it with staples. Cut a piece of lining fabric for the lid with a 5cm (2in) allowance all round. Attach it to the front edge of the lid using a back tacking strip to create a neat edge. Before stapling it, position a small loop of ribbon in the centre to act as a lip to open the lid. Cut a layer of wadding to sit 2.5cm (1in) inside the lid frame. Using the staple gun, attach it to the back tacking strip.

step 20 Take the lining fabric across the lid, over the back tacking strip, to the back edge and fold it under, creating a straight line along the edge. Use pins to secure it to the suede. Pin the two remaining edges in the same way and then carefully slip stitch around these three sides.

step 21 Attach a dust cloth to the underside of the box and then reattach the legs, in this case screwing them back in to the base. Offer up the lid to the box and screw the hinges back in place on the lid. Trim the lengths of keeper ribbon so that they will keep the lid in the desired position when open, adding an allowance for attaching them. Attach them to the lid with two studs, taking care to position them in the right spot. Using the glue gun, add a few decorative velvet flowers to the box as the finishing touches.

ottoman

This piece was originally an old French day bed with a pair of arms that could be angled, laid flat, or taken off completely. We discarded them as they were in very poor condition, leaving us the base which was a great opportunity to show off a stunning cowhide (a rich-coloured velvet would also show off its angles well). Fairly large antique-finish studs were chosen to complete the piece. It is best to select your own hide, rather than ordering one without seeing it: while none are perfect, some are far more attractive than others. A good balance of white, brown, and black works well, and shorter hair is more appealing than long. Where possible buy a whole hide and, when choosing it, look carefully for any holes or marks. Make sure your supplier can guarantee that the hide is a by-product.

tools
Craft knife, magnetic hammer, scissors, staple gun (optional).

materials
20mm (¾in) decorative studs, dust cloth, masking tape, 16mm (⅝in) tacks, top fabric.

reference
Cuts, corners, and folds: pp158–9.

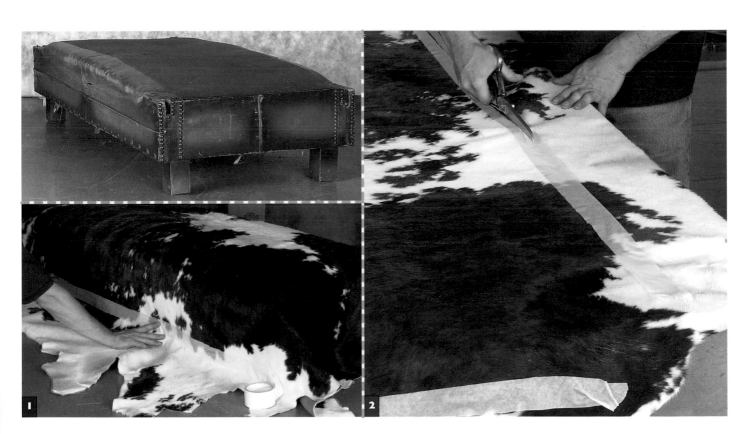

step 1 Strip the old covering and re-cover with cotton felt and calico. Choose the best part of the hide with the strongest pattern. With the right side facing up, decide how you want the hide to lie (here, the spine runs down the centre of the ottoman); use masking tape to show where to cut the hide, making an allowance of 10cm (4in) beyond the base rails of the ottoman. Make sure the hide is "the right way up", so the pile feels smooth when you run your hand from the back of the piece to the front.

step 2 Place the hide on a large work surface or clean floor so it can lie flat. Wear old clothing when working with hides: they shed a surprising amount of hair and you and the surrounding area could get covered. Cut the hide down the centre of the masking tape to help limit the amount of hair that falls away. Take your time when cutting as a mistake cannot be easily rectified and could prove costly.

step 3 Put the hide back on the ottoman, ensuring its position is absolutely as you wish. Attach it with a centre tack on the underside of each of the side rails. Pull it taut across the top of the ottoman as it will give and become more supple over time. Working your way from the centre tacks out to the corners, place spaced tacks, leaving 8cm (3in) free on each side of the corners. As you work, continue to pull the hide taut from side to side and end to end.

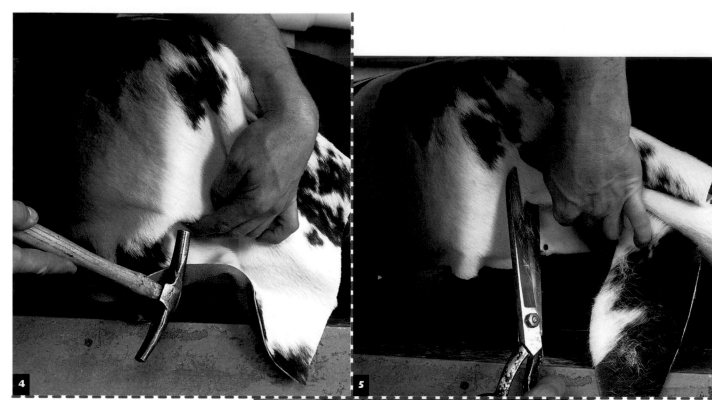

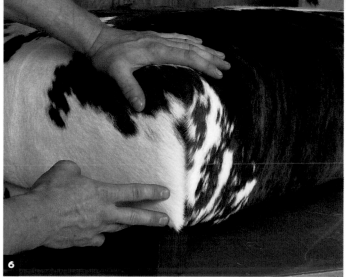

step 4 To secure the corners, pull the hide across one corner and secure on the underside with a tack on the other side.

step 5 Now make a cut within the corner fold to reduce the layers of thick hide on the corners, making sure you cut the excess on the inside of the fold.

step 6 Pull the hide back to the corner and fold it under creating a neat, straight line down the length of the corner. Secure it with tacks on the underside of the rails. Tack the hide securely in place on the underside, ready for the dust cloth to be attached. Repeat this on each of the three remaining corners.

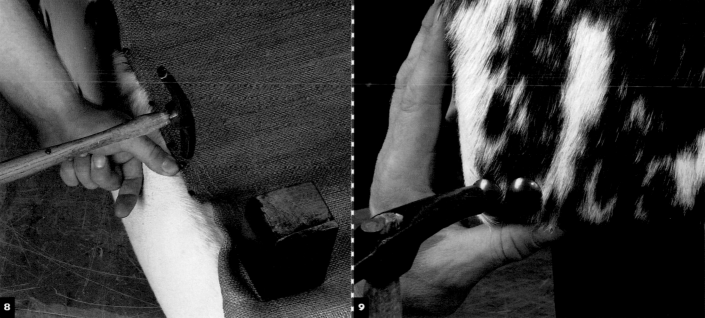

step 7 Measure and cut the dust cloth with a 8cm (3in) allowance. Place it over the underside of the frame. At each leg, make a large X-shaped cut (the size of leg) and gently pull the cloth over the leg. Tuck under the triangular shapes that are left, so that they are inside the dust cloth.

step 8 Place a centre tack in each of the rails on the underside of the frame, turning the cloth under as you work. Make sure the cloth is pulled relatively taut to avoid it sagging over time. Working out from the centre tacks, secure the edges and the corners of the dust cloth in the normal way.

step 9 Attach the decorative studs, working from the corners out and ensuring their bottom edge lines up with the bottom of the ottoman. Carefully place each stud beside its predecessor so their edges just touch. Hammer the studs in their centre, gently working them into the piece, taking care not to dent the sides or dome.

70s "flower" stool

This distinctive footstool was originally made in the 1970s by a company called Sherborne and was accompanied by a rather fabulous chair. The circular centre surrounded by triangular segments produces a flower-like shape very reminscent of the character of the chair's era, which we have taken further by upholstering it in a luscious lime green velvet. The outline of each segment is picked out in rich dark green piping, giving gentle emphasis to its shape. The aluminium base, with its simple lines echoing the flower image, lends the piece a contemporary look; before being reattached, it was polished to regain some of its original sparkle. This is a relatively straightforward piece to upholster, however, precision and patience is needed to get the piping to sit in exactly the right position around the top of each segment.

tools
Bread knife, craft knife, marker pen, sewing machine, scissors, screwdriver, staple gun, tape measure, wooden rule.

materials
Piping cord, polyester wadding, reflex foam (two thicknesses, see step 2), spray adhesive, tailor's chalk, top fabric.

reference
Applying single piping: p74, making and joining single piping: pp162–3.

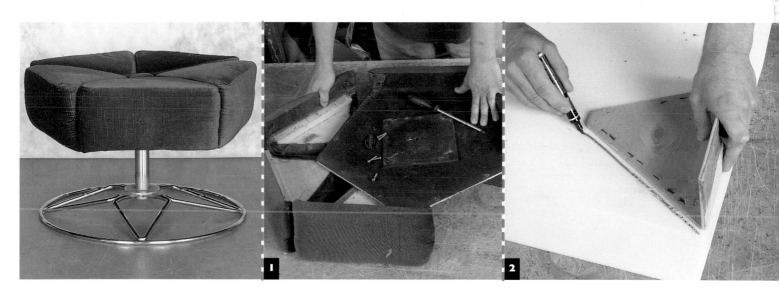

Before embarking on a project such as this it is worthwhile bearing in mind that often the smaller the piece of furniture, the harder it is to work on. This stool is made more complex by the single piping attached to the top panels of fabric, especially as each panel has three corners on it. Small does not necessarily mean easy!

step 1 Remove the aluminium base of the stool using a screwdriver. Unscrew the metal base holding the five padded segments together and carefully remove the old fabric. If the old foam needs to be replaced, which is advisable in order to ensure that you are using fire retardant foam, remove this too. This should leave five wooden platforms, each with a piece of wood on the outside – the bases to which the foam and fabric are attached.

step 2 Use one of the wooden platforms as a template for cutting out the replacement foam. Place the triangular part on the foam, mark out the shape, and then cut it out using a bread knife. Make the foam piece a fraction larger than the platform – no more than 1cm (⅜in) – so that it fits snugly inside the fitted cover. Choose foam of a similar depth to the original. Attach the foam pieces to the top surface of the wooden platforms using spray adhesive. In the same way, cut out pieces of foam for the wooden sides; for these use thinner foam, approximately 1cm (⅜in). Attach them to the outside of the wood sides.

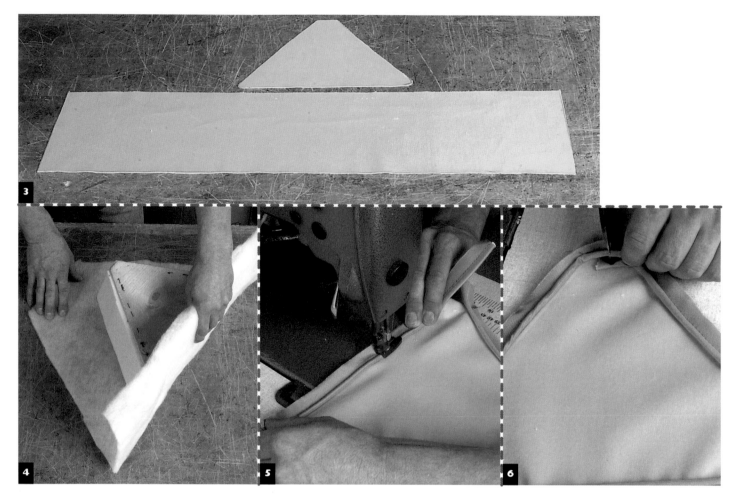

step 3 Place a foam block (glued to its wooden platform) on to the underside of the top fabric and draw around the triangular shape with tailor's chalk. Cut it out with an allowance of 1cm (⅜in) all round. Cut the side panel of fabric as one piece: measure the circumference and depth of one of the foam shapes and, using tailor's chalk and a wooden rule, mark these measurements on the underside of the fabric (the depth should be that of the wooden side panel). Cut the panel out with a 2.5cm (1in) allowance. Make marks with tailor's chalk to indicate the finished shape and size of the segment against the extra allowance. Repeat this process for each of the five segments.

step 4 Cut polyester wadding to cover the foam on the top and sides of each of the segments, with an allowance of 2cm (¾in) at the bottom. Using spray adhesive on both the foam and the wadding, carefully wrap the wadding around the foam block securing it in place. Trim away any excess wadding from around the edges of the foam.

step 5 Prepare the piping to go around the top of each of the segments (see page 74 and 163 for making and applying piping). Sew the piping to the top panel of fabric in one length beginning just to the side of the apex of the triangle (where the segment will meet the centre of the stool). Place the piping on the good side of the top fabric along the tailor's chalk markings made earlier (step 3) and with both raw edges lined up, machine-stitch along one side, around the corner at the outside of the triangle, along the back section, around the second corner and then along the remaining side to the starting point, leaving a small gap of 2.5cm (1in) here. At each corner, make small cuts in the piping hem to help it lie neatly.

step 6 Carefully butt together the two ends of piping (see page 162 for further details on how to do this). This is a relatively tricky process so take your time. Repeat steps 5 and 6 for each top panel of fabric.

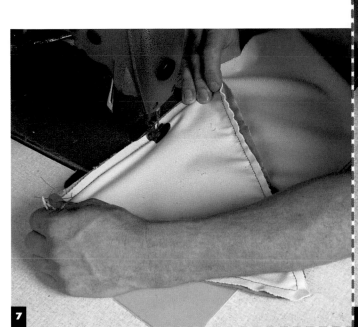

step 7 With the piping in place, the top panel can now be attached to the side panel fabric. Lay the apex of the triangle, where the piping was joined, at one end of the side panel fabric – good sides facing each other. Using the sewing machine, attach one side of the top panel to the side panel fabric. At the corner, lay the following side against the edge of the side panel of fabric and continue sewing round: you are effectively creating a triangular-shaped tube to slot over the foam block. Continue to the remaining corner and then back to the apex so that all sides of the top panel are attached to the side panel.

step 8 Join the ends of the side panel together to finish the tube shape: line up the two edges of fabric, good sides facing, and machine-stitch together, making sure you follow the markings made with the tailor's chalk. Start where the seam meets the top panel and sew down to the open end at the bottom. Now turn the tube the right way out with the seams inside and stretch the line of piping along the top, ensuring it lies straight and taut. Repeat steps 7 and 8 on each of the segments.

step 9 Cut sufficient foam for the round centre of the stool, using the old foam as a reference. Prepare the piping and fabric cover following the same process as for the five segments (steps 3–8). Turn the fabric tube the right way out and carefully insert the tube of foam.

step 10 Fit each triangular cover to a segment, carefully manipulating it over the foam and wood block so the piping lies exactly along the horizontal edges on the top of the block. At each of the outside corners, make a cut in the hem of the fabric so it can be fitted around the side panel of

wood. Take it over the lip of wood and secure it to the inside of the side panel using a staple gun. Attach it at the apex of the triangle and along the base with neat staples.

step 11 Once all the segments are complete, align each piece on the wooden base and screw them back on. Then screw the aluminium base in place.

footstool with fitted cover

A contemporary round footstool is a useful piece of furniture, providing additional colour, supplementing existing furniture, or completing the look by adding another shape and point of interest. The plain round shape of this stool is easy to work with and there are only two surfaces to cover: the top and the side. In this case, a fitted cover produces a clean and neat finish and, is a simple exercise. This bold orange velvet has a raised geometric print, contrasting with the circular shape of the stool. The stool was new and came upholstered in calico; the original legs were metal, which we have replaced with hand polished, rich wood ones.

tools
Scissors, sewing machine, staple gun, tailor's chalk, tape measure.

materials
Dust cloth, staples, sewing machine thread, top fabric.

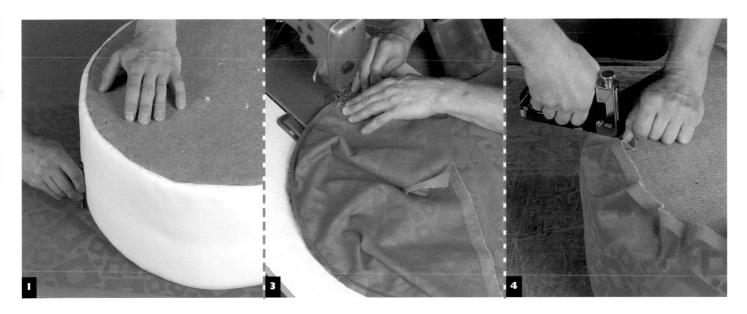

step 1 Remove the four legs by simply unscrewing them from the base and put them to one side. Lay the top fabric on your work surface, right side up, and place the footstool upside down on it. Draw around the shape. Cut out the shape with a 1.5cm (⅝in) allowance all round.

step 2 Taking the tape measure all the way round the sides of the stool, measure the circumference and measure the height of the pad. Mark up the dimensions on the fabric and cut out the length of fabric with a 1.5cm (⅝in) allowance all round.

step 3 Place the circular panel at one end of the side panel, good sides facing each other, and pin along the edge. Using the sewing machine, sew along the chalk markings, making a small hem. Trim away the excess fabric. Now sew the seam in the side panel, good sides of the fabric facing each other.

step 4 Turn the cover the right way out and carefully manipulate it over the stool. Smooth it across the top and down the sides, then secure it underneath with four centre staples. Working out from each of these centre staples, gradually place more staples, making folds in the fabric to secure it neatly. All the staples should be placed approximately 2.5cm (1in) from the edge of the stool. Ensure the fabric lies taut across the top of the stool and down the sides. Trim away any excess fabric.

step 5 Cut sufficient dust cloth to cover the underside of the stool with a 2cm (¾in) allowance all round. Place the cloth over the underside and, turning it under so it lies approximately 1cm (½in) in from the edges of the stool, place four centre staples. Make a small hole in the cloth where each of the legs will be screwed in. Add more staples working from the centre one out until the exercise is complete. Screw the wooden legs back into the base.

footstool with loose cover

This is the same simple stool as the previous one, but this alternative treatment reveals how a quite different look can be easily achieved. This time a loose cover has been made and, in order to obtain a crisp, structured finish, the top fabric has been lined with fire retardant barrier cloth. The circular shapes on this beautiful duck-egg blue fabric echo the shape of the stool and the plain brown suede piping provides definition while also mirroring the brown patterns on the fabric and the brown wood of the feet. A loose cover is more easily cleaned and allows for a number of different covers so that they can change with the season.

tools
Scissors, sewing machine, tailor's chalk, tape measure.

materials
Barrier cloth, piping cord, sheet of plastic, sewing machine thread, top fabric.

reference
Applying/making piping: p74 and p163.

step 1 Begin by working out how and where the pattern of the fabric will lie on the top of the stool. To make this easier, cut out a template of the stool shape using a piece of clear plastic and place this over the good side of the fabric. Using tailor's chalk, draw around the plastic and cut the fabric with a 1.5cm (⅝in) allowance all round. Measure around the sides of the stool and its height and cut out the fabric with the same allowance. Use your judgement to decide how long the sides of the cover should be; here it reaches to 6cm (2½in) from the bottom of the legs. Cut out the same dimensions in the lining cloth. Unscrew the legs from the base.

step 2 Prepare two lengths of single piping to go around the top and bottom of the cover. Position a length of piping on the good side of the side panel of fabric, the raw edge of the piping lying along the edge of the fabric. If you are using a pattern attach the piping to the bottom edge of the side panel first. Carefully sew these together with the sewing machine. Making small cuts into the hem of the piping will help it sit more easily around the curves.

step 3 Place this panel, good side down, over the lining cloth so the piping is sandwiched between the two, and line up the edges. Carefully sew the two pieces of fabric together, taking care that when they are folded back the piping will be visible, neatly positioned between the two.

step 4 Fold the two pieces back so the wrong side of the top fabric now lies against the lining.

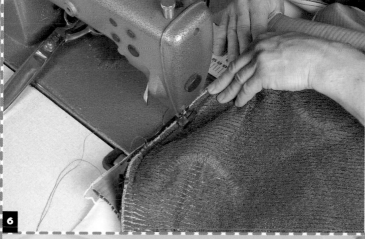

step 5 Carry out the same process for the top panel of fabric, attaching the single piping to the good side of the fabric. Again make small cuts to the raw edge of the piping as you sew as this will allow it to lie better around the curves. Carefully butt together the two ends of piping (see page 74), trimming away any excess piping and fabric. Attach the lining in the same way as for the side panel.

step 6 Place the good side of the top panel onto the good side of the side panel so the edges line up and, taking your time, sew these together.

step 7 With the good side of the fabric still facing in, sew together the two ends of the side panel, forming a tube. Take care to butt together the two ends of piping around the base of the side panel and trim away any excess fabric and piping.

step 8 Screw the wooden legs back into the base and, turning the cover the right side out, fit it over the stool, smoothing the piping around the top.

screen

This three-panelled screen is relatively straightforward to make from scratch using a man-made material such as plywood. You may, however, prefer to re-cover an old screen, which typically will consist of a framework of wood battons, making it lighter to work with. When assembling the screen, care should be taken to ensure the panels are positioned in the right order. The panels on one side of this screen are upholstered in a stunning fabric that has lime-green and mushroom-coloured velvet flock on a linen base; on the reverse of each panel is a plain but luxurious silk, offering three different textures. The trimming is a simple ribbon in a similar green to the velvet flock. With the plywood screen it is appropriate to use a staple gun as all the materials are new, the staples will allow a neater, more precise finish, and are quicker to position. With an old screen you might prefer to maintain the integrity of the piece and use tacks instead. With plywood the hinges are best secured to the flat surface of the panels.

tools
Craft knife, hot-glue gun, pencil, jigsaw, scissors, staple gun, wooden rule.

materials
Cardboard, glue sticks, hinges (three pairs), plywood, polyester wadding, ribbon, spray adhesive, staples, top fabric (two designs).

reference
Applying braid and ribbon: p72.

2

3

step 1 If you are working on an old screen, remove any old tacks or staples and the old hinges, leaving a clean, smooth surface to work on. To make the screen from scratch first decide on the size and shape of the panels – the panels here are 2m (6ft) high by 50cm (20in) wide.

step 2 To achieve a symmetrical curve at the top of the screen, create a template of the desired shape on cardboard. Draw half of the template on card; this is then flipped horizontally on the plywood to create the other half. To do this, first begin by drawing an oblong shape roughly 20cm (8in) wide

and 30cm (12in) high and beside this draw the shape of the screen curve, remember to draw only half the shape, this will give it a straight edge. Now draw two straight lines in the desired screen width on to the plywood and place the cut out shape lining up the straight edges. Draw around the template and then flip it horizontally and draw around it to create the other half. Draw a line at the bottom to indicate the base of the screen.

step 3 Use a jigsaw to cut around the shape. When all the panels have been cut, use the rule and pencil to mark the hinge positions. Place the hinges over these marks and pencil in where the screws will go. Depending on whether it is an old or new screen, the hinges can be positioned either on the outside edges of the panels or directly on to the flat surface. In this case they are going on the back surface. Screw in the hinges on each of the two outer panels.

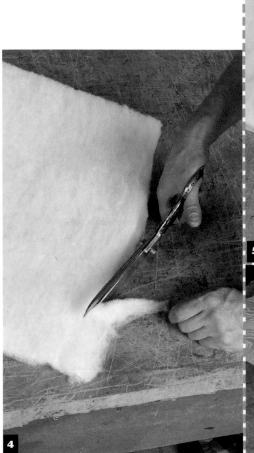

step 4 Place a strip of polyester wadding on one side of each panel and, using a pair of scissors, carefully trim around the shape so the wadding fits the panel exactly.

step 5 Glue the wadding into place using spray adhesive. Starting at the top, spray the adhesive onto the board and carefully smooth the wadding back into place. Work down the length of the panel. Repeat on the remaining two panels. Turn the panels over and repeat the process, cutting and attaching polyester wadding to each panel. Another layer of polyester wadding can be added to each side to give more depth and shape if required. On the middle panel, br careful not to glue the area around where the hinges will be attached.

step 6 Cut the fabric for the reverse of each panel with a 2.5cm (1in) allowance all round. Place one piece on the reverse side of a panel, smoothing it into place. Initially, hold it in place with a staple in the centre of each outside edge. Then, working out from each centre staple, secure the fabric with more staples, continually smoothing it out. Take care around each corner, making small, neat folds and securing these with staples. Fold the fabric under beside the hinges. Trim away any excess fabric around the panel. Repeat this exercise on each of the panels, leaving the fabric around the hinge positions on the middle panel unattached.

step 7 Cut sufficient top fabric for the front of each panel with a 2.5cm (1in) allowance all round. If you are using a patterned fabric, take care where the pattern will sit on each panel so they will match up. Marking the panels – a, b, and c – with masking tape will help you in this process. Folding the fabric under, place a centre staple on each of the four outer edges of the panel as before.

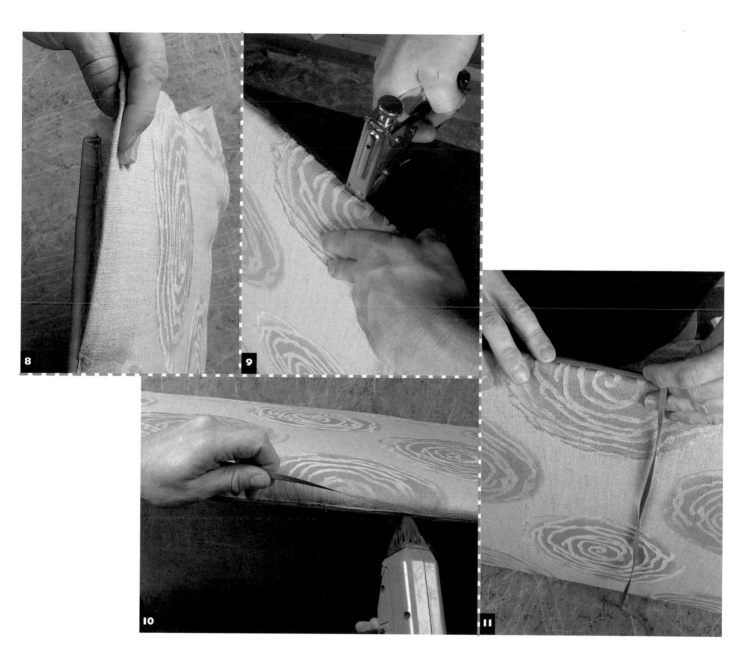

step 8 Folding the fabric under, continue to place more staples, working from the centre out towards each corner.

step 9 Smooth the fabric across the panel, ensuring the fabric lies absolutely flat and the weave is straight. As the fabric is smoothed down, it will naturally pull the wadding underneath over each edge, which will cover any sharp edges in the plywood. Take care around each corner, making small, neat folds and securing these with staples. Repeat for the other two panels.

step 10 Apply the ribbon trimming to the two outer panels. Begin by attaching it to the underside at the base of the panel so the join will not be visible. Place a little adhesive at one end of the ribbon, fold it under by 1cm (⅜in), then attach it, pressing it firmly in place.

step 11 Carefully apply glue along the edges of the first panel, keeping a straight line, then work the ribbon along each edge, positioning it over the line of glue and making sure it covers the line of staples and the edge of the fabric. Press it down firmly with your fingers as you go. Apply the ribbon to the other outer panel. Now secure the hinges to the centre panel, and then carefully fold and glue the fabric in place. Attach the trimming to the centre panel, carefully butting together the two pieces of ribbon to the underside of the panel.

shaped headboard

A headboard frames the top end of a bed, adding structure and definition, and also making the bed a more comfortable piece of furniture. It is amazing the impact that a headboard can have in a bedroom, adding decoration through its size, shape, colour, and texture. A simple rectangular headboard will sit well in a contemporary space, blending in with other modern shapes in a bedroom, whereas a more ornate, curved, and shaped headboard can have a more sensuous and glamorous effect. This headboard has a simple curved shape that is accentuated by the fabric with its delicate golden swirls on a midnight-black background. Single piping around the edges further defines and accentuates the curves. Two small velvet cushions in another shade of black add the finishing touches to the bed as a whole and produce a perfect balance with the headboard.

tools
Jigsaw, pencil, scissors, screwdriver, sewing machine, staple gun, wood rule.

materials
Cardboard, dust cloth, 2cm (¾in) foam, keyhole wall brackets (two), mdf, piping cord, polyester wadding, spray adhesive, staples, top fabric.

reference
Applying single piping: p74, shaping a board: pp146–9, making and joining single piping: pp162–3.

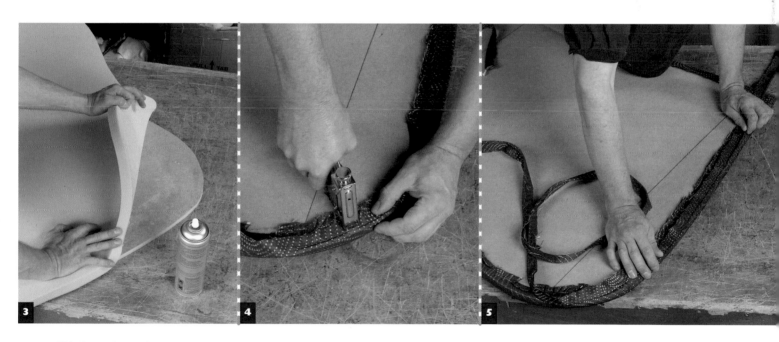

step 1 Work out the ideal size by measuring the width of the bed frame and adding 8cm (3in) each side; in this case the highest point of the headboard should be about 97cm (38in) from the base of the mattress.

step 2 To gain a symmetrical shape on the top of the board, create a template by drawing half of the curved shape onto cardboard (see page 147, steps 2 and 3). If the mdf board is not wide enough to fit the whole headboard, make it from three pieces with the centre piece the widest. Cut out the mdf with a jigsaw and, if appropriate, glue the pieces together with wood glue.

step 3 Using the cardboard template, cut sufficient foam to cover one side of the headboard with a 1cm (⅜in) allowance. Attach this to the mdf with spray adhesive. Add a layer of polyester wadding, taking it around to the back of the board and attaching it with four centre staples.

step 4 Cut sufficient top fabric to cover one side of the headboard with an 8cm (3in) allowance all round. Position the fabric, take it round and over the sides, and attach it to the back of the board, placing a staple in the centre along the sides, top, and bottom – no more than 2cm (¾in) in from the edges.

Ensuring the fabric lies straight with good tension, gradually add more staples working from the centre staples out. Where the curved shape bends inwards make small cuts in the fabric on the back of the board to allow it to lie flat, without cutting too deep. Around each of the bottom corners, make a simple fold in the fabric and secure it with staples.

step 5 Make the single piping (see page 163). There should be enough to go around the sides and top of the headboard with a 10cm (4in) allowance. Place the piping on the back of the headboard, just around the edge so it can be seen from the front.

step 6 With the headboard lying flat on the work surface, begin attaching the piping to the headboard starting in a bottom corner and folding the end under to secure it. Working your way up the side of the board, place the staples snugly below the piping ensuring it sits proud around the edge. Continue until you reach the other bottom corner. Secure the end by folding it over.

step 7 Cut sufficient dust cloth to cover the back of the board with a 5cm (2in) allowance. We have used a complementary black dust cloth but any strong plain cotton can be used instead. Place the cloth over the back of the headboard and make small cuts to allow it to fit around the concave curves. Take care not to cut too deeply – only to where the staples will be placed.

step 8 Fold under the edges of the dust cloth so they lie just below the line of piping, making a neat tidy fit.

step 9 Using the staple gun, place three centre staples along the top and sides of the back of the headboard. Gradually place more staples, working from the centre staples out and taking care that the folded fabric lies snug against the underside of the piping. Place the staples close along the line of the fold.

step 10 Trim away any excess fabric around each of the corners to make the fold less bulky.

step 11 Fold the fabric under itself creating a neat fold at the corner, making sure it follows the line of the board underneath. Secure both of the bottom corner folds with two staples along each side of the fold.

step 12 Using a wood rule, measure 20cm (8in) in from each of the sides and 15cm (6in) down from the top of the board and make a mark where each of the two keyhole brackets will be secured. Fasten the brackets with a screwdriver. They should be absolutely tight against the board so that they can carry the considerable weight of the board when it hangs on the wall. If you have used more than one piece of mdf take care to avoid the join when placing the brackets.

step 13 Measure and mark the points above the bed where the corresponding screws will be attached. Secure the screws to the wall and then gently place the headboard over these, securing it in place.

panelled headboard

This style of headboard is rather more opulent and creates a very strong impact. It would work well in a room with high ceilings. There are two parts to this headboard (one smaller padded board sits inside the other) offering the opportunity to combine different fabrics. Here, a plain oyster silk is complemented by a sumptuous silk in a similar colour but with a delicate pattern in silver print; the overall effect is wonderfully luxurious without being overbearing. Simple piping frames the inset panel, giving it subtle definition. Deciding on the size and shape of headboard and ensuring the proportions are right is not always easy. If you are unsure, a template of your proposed shape and design can be drawn out on some old wallpaper and temporarily secured above the bed to give you a better idea.

tools
Saw, large needle, pencil, scissors, screwdriver, sewing machine, staple gun, wood rule.

materials
Cardboard, dust cloth, 2cm (¾in) and 5cm (2in) foam, 2 keyhole wall brackets, mdf, piping cord, polyester wadding, spray adhesive, staples, thread, top fabric.

reference
Applying/making piping: p74 and pp162–3.

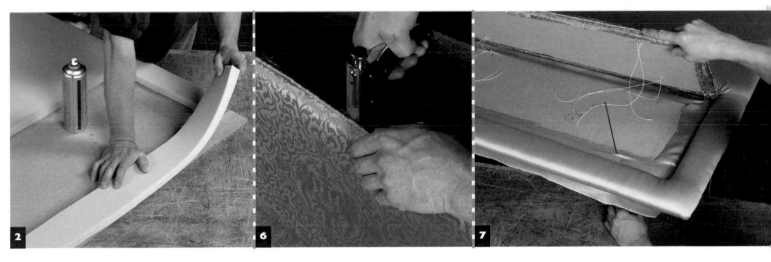

step 1 This board is 156cm (61½in) square. The panel is 140cm (55in) by 38cm (15in) and sits within the larger board, with an 8cm (3in) border on each side. Make the headboard to suit the size of your bed. Measure and cut the mdf, then draw in the outline of the panel.

step 2 With a 1cm (⅜in) allowance all round, cut sufficient foam to cover the main board to the base of the inset panel and then cut three pieces to go around the sides and above the panel. Attach the foam to the headboard using spray adhesive. Now add a layer of polyester wadding, taking it around the edges to the back of the board and securing it with staples. Cut out the wadding around the space left for the panel.

step 3 Cut sufficient fabric to cover the front of the board with an 8cm (3in)

allowance. If two pieces of fabric need to be joined to cover the whole board, choose an inconspicuous place for the join and machine-sew them together. Attach the fabric to the back of the board with a staple in the centre of each side and along the top and bottom. Add more staples from the centres out, ensuring the fabric is taut and straight on the front. Measure and cut out a hole in the fabric where the panel will sit, leaving a 5cm (2in) allowance. Staple it around the panel hole, close to the foam border.

step 4 In a top corner of the inset panel, about 8cm (3in) in from the top and 12cm (5in) in from the side, drill a pair of holes, 1cm (⅜in) apart. Repeat at each corner. Using a large needle, thread 50cm (20in) of string through each pair of holes so the ends come out at the back. Now drill four pairs of corresponding holes in the main board.

step 5 Cut to size and attach the foam and wadding to the inset panel and then cut and attach the fabric to it in the same way as the main headboard.

step 6 Make single piping to go around the panel with a 5cm (2in) allowance. Staple this in place along the outside edges of the inset panel so that it sits proud and can be seen when in position. Trim the ends of piping so they butt neatly together.

step 7 Carefully slot the inset panel into the space on the main board and use a needle to thread the string on the panel through the holes on the main board. Secure the string on the back of the headboard with plenty of staples. Attach the dust cloth with staples, turngin it under, then screw the keyhole brackets to the back of the board and place the corresponding screws on the wall.

reference

cuts, corners, and folds

There are many cuts and folds in the upholstery process and the key to a secure foundation and a tidy finish is to make them cleanly and neatly at each stage. Take care not to make any of the cuts too deep, cutting in only as far as necessary. The majority of folds are held in place with tacks, staples, or gimp pins; however, in some cases, they are further secured with slip stitching (such as on the button-back chair on page 98 for example). When making folds around corners, trim away any excess fabric from within the fold to avoid any bulkiness or untidy outlines.

cuts

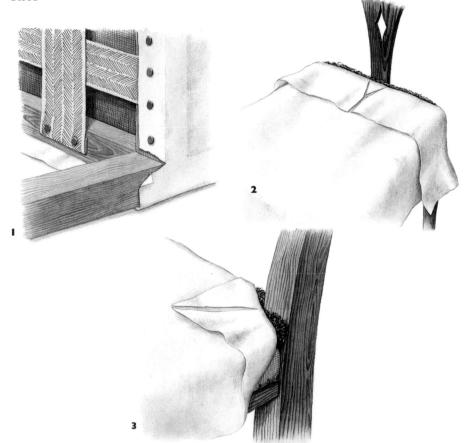

pleating on a rounded corner

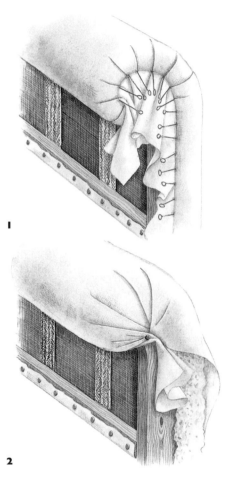

I staight cut This is a cut that is made in a straight line allowing the fabric to be taken in different directions.

2 Y cut This allows the fabric to be fitted around three sides of a rail or upright. Pull the fabric away from the upright, folding it back over itself, and make a straight cut in towards the centre of the upright, stopping no closer than 2cm (¾in) from the upright; now make two small diagonal cuts from

here towards each side of the upright. Fold the centre flap under itself and pull the remaining fabric either side of the upright.

3 T cut This cut allows the fabric to fit around two sides of an upright. Pull the fabric away from the upright, folding it back over itself, then make a diagonal cut towards the facing corner of the upright. Fold the fabric down each side of the upright.

pleat I For a neat, uniform look around a curve, make a series of folds around it, working from the centre out, holding each pleat in place with a skewer. Aim to make each fold the same size so that you achieve an even balance. Secure each pleat to the arm facing with stitching or tacks.

pleat 2 For an informal look, begin by making a pleat in the centre of the curve, pull the fabric down, and secure it with a tack. Continue to make more pleats, working from the centre out to the sides of the curve, pulling the fabric into the middle of the arm facing and securing with tacks.

folds
making a fold around a front corner

I

2

3

folds
making two folds around a front corner

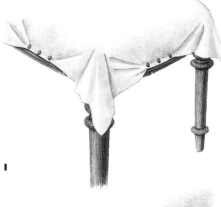

I

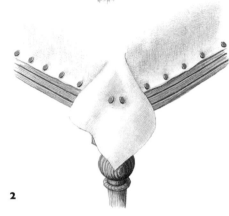

2

3

folds
folding around a back upright

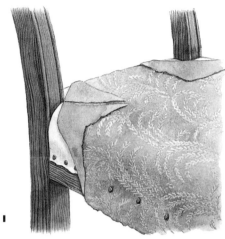

I

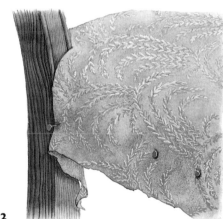

2

step I Take the fabric from the side rail, wrap it around the corner to the front rail (which is on the left in the picture), and secure with a tack. Take the fabric from the front rail and fold it under itself to create a crease on the corner.

step 2 Open out the crease to reveal a V-shape in the fabric. Trim away the excess fabric inside the V.

step 3 Fold the remaining fabric under again ensuring there is a neat fold down the length of the corner and secure with a tack.

step I Place tacks to within 5cm (2in) of the corner, trimming away any excess cotton felt around the corner.

step 2 Pull the fabric down over the point of the corner and secure the fabric on each side of the corner with a tack.

step 3 Trim away any excess fabric and then take the loose fabric on either side of the corner and fold it into the corner point, securing with a tack.

step I Pull the fabric back and make a T cut (see cuts opposite).

step 2 Pull each flap of fabric down either side of the upright and trim away the excess. Turn the fabric under itself to create a neat fold that fits snugly down each side of the upright and secure with a tack.

stitches

Stitches are an important part of upholstering: they provide strength and stability during the stuffing process, help to secure one piece of fabric to another, and, on some occasions, have a decorative role too. It is important to create stitching that is both neat and secure. In particular, slip stitching, which is used on top fabric, needs to be tidy, as any badly placed stitches will be very obvious on the finished piece.

wall stitch (blind stitch)

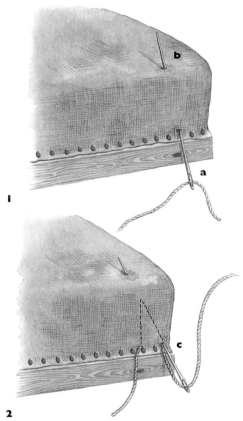

1

2

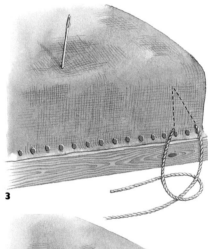

3

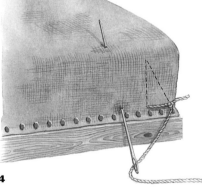

4

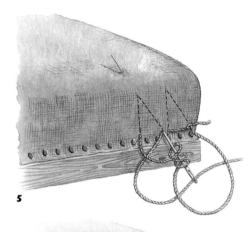

5

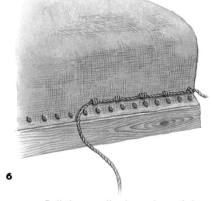

6

step 1 The wall stitch helps create a firm wall of stuffing along the sides of a seat pad, arm, or inside back. Take a long double-ended needle and push it into the stuffing, just above the tack line working from the right side of the frame to the left (a). Push the needle in at an angle, aiming for it to appear on the top of the pad 5cm (2in) in from the front edge of the seat (b).

step 2 Do not bring the needle out entirely. When you begin to see its eye, push it back in, scooping it around the stuffing and angling it so that it comes out approximately 2cm (¾in) to the right of where it initially went in (c).

step 3 Remove the needle and rest it in the top of the seat pad while you make a slip knot with the two lengths of twine at the tack line.

step 4 Re-thread the needle and push it back in 4cm (1½in) along from the slip knot, again at an angle.

step 5 Pull the needle through until the eye is just below the surface, scoop it around the fibre as you push it back down to the tack line, this time bringing it only halfway out. Loop the twine around the needle three times (see photo "b" opposite) before bringing the needle out completely, taking it through the loops. Lock the knot by pulling it to the right and left until it tightens, and you can feel the fibre being pulled closer to the edge.

step 6 Continue this stitch along each edge of the pad. At the end fasten the twine off by wrapping both lengths of it around the needle three times and locking it tight.

roll stitch (top stitch)

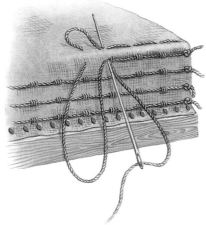

a **roll stitch** (see photo "c") helps create a firm edge. It begins like wall stitch but when you push the needle into the side of the pad, you bring it out completely on the top. Then, reinsert it, threaded end first, 2cm (¾in) back along the top, making a visible stitch. Continue pushing it back down through the side of the pad bringing it out along the front edge. Proceed as for the wall stitch.

blanket stitch

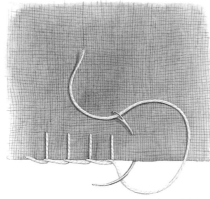

blanket stitch secures one edge of fabric to another and is done with a semi-circular needle. Secure the thread and make a stitch along the edge of the fabric. As the needle point comes out of the fabric, take the thread around the back of the needle, and then pull the needle through, so the stitch sits along the edge of the fabric, continue on to the next stitch.

a creating a slip knot at the start of bridle ties (see step I, bridle ties, p162)

b looping the twine around the needle in wall stitch (see step 5, wall stitch, p160)

c roll stitch (see top left)

bridle ties

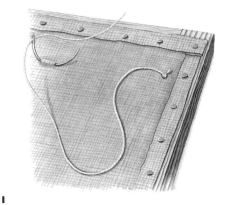

1

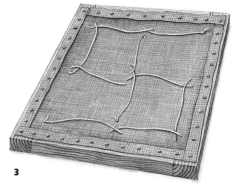

2

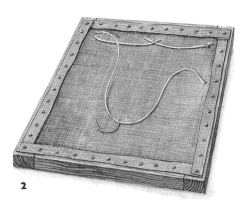

3

back stitch

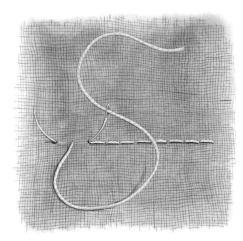

back stitch is a strong hand-sewn stitch used to hold fabric together. Insert the needle then bring it out twice as far along the row as the stitch length before reinserting it at the end of the last stitch.

slip stitch

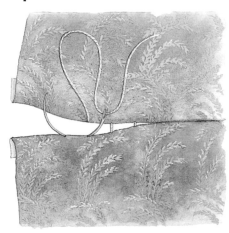

slip stitch is a hand stitch used to sew two pieces of fabric together creating an invisible seam on a piece of furniture. With the top fabric folded under, draw the two pieces of fabric together, stitching along the seam line, making sure the stitches are hidden. Begin each stitch opposite the last.

single piping

1

2

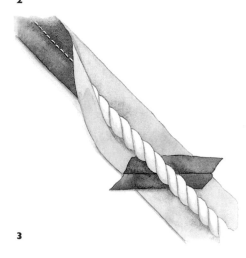

3

step 1 Bridle ties are a series of loops made in hessian to hold stuffing in place. Make a slip knot in one corner (see photo "a", p161) then stitch a loop 10cm (4in) long, reinserting the needle to make a 1cm (⅜in) backstitch. Each loop should be big enough to put your hand under when adding the stuffing.

step 2 Working your way around and across the pad, continue to make loops.

step 3 At the end tie off the twine with a double slip knot. Add more rows if necessary, beginning each with a slip knot.

step 1 Cut strips of fabric approximately 4cm (1½in) in width along the bias, cutting the ends on the diagonal.

step 2 Pin two strips together with the good sides facing in, as in the diagram, matching the pattern if appropriate. Sew this seam (indicated by the pin on the diagram) on a sewing machine.

step 3 Lay piping cord down the length of fabric and wrap the fabric around it, with the good side of the fabric facing out. Proceed to step 4 to seal the fabric around the piping cord.

single saddle stitch

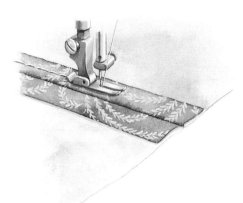

double piping

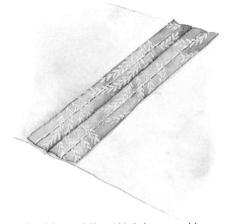

1

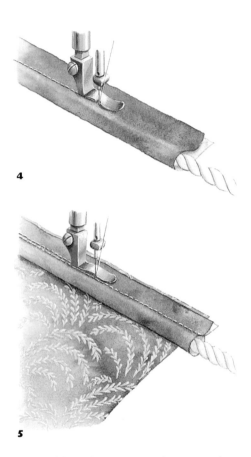

4

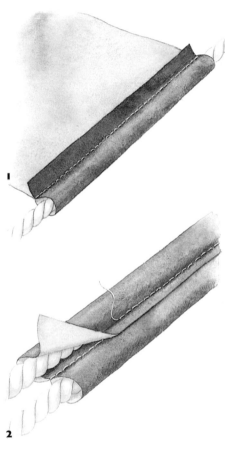

5

2

single saddle stitch is a decorative stitch, adding interest to an otherwise plain seam. Join two lengths of fabric using the sewing machine and leaving a 2cm (¾in) hem. Press down the hem so it lies flat on either side of the seam, then sew down one length of hem.

double saddle stitch

double saddle stitch is created by carrying out the same process as for single saddle stitch but with the addition of a second row of stitching along the opposite hem.

step 4 Using the sewing maching, sew a line of stitching close to the cord. A piping or zip foot on a medium stitch setting is useful.

step 5 Lay the single piping along the good side of the piece of fabric you wish to attach it to. Ensure the raw edges of the piping seam line up with the raw edge of the fabric before stitching the two together.

step 1 Cut a length of fabric 5cm (2in) wide if possible, again on the bias. Lay it good side down and place the first length of cord along one side of it. Fold the fabric over so it encases the cord and make a line of stitches the length of the cord with the sewing machine. Ensure the stitches are close to the cord.

step 2 Take the second length of cord and lay this on the reverse side of the fabric, beside the first length. Fold the fabric over the piping cord and carefully sew between the two lengths of piping, over the first line of stitching.

knots

There are a number of basic knots that are used frequently in upholstery. Each knot is suitable for different situations but, in time, you will work out which you prefer to use and what works best for you.

slip knot

I

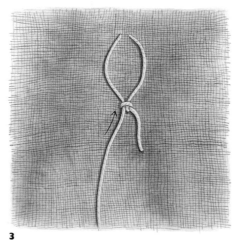

3

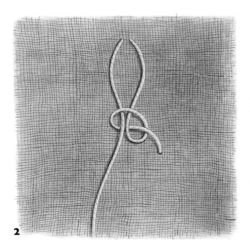

2

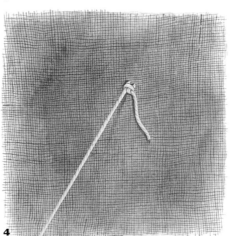

4

half hitch knot

hitch knot

locking/single knot

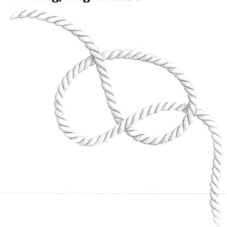

step 1 Make a stitch with twine. Holding the two loose ends of twine together, make a loop with the right-hand one then take the end of it over both pieces of twine.

step 2 Take this same length of twine under both pieces of twine and through the loop on the right.

step 3 Pull the same length of twine to tighten the knot, ready for it to be slipped down in the direction of the arrow.

step 4 Holding onto the longer piece of twine, slip the knot down so it rests against the fabric.

half hitch knot Take the cord over the spring wire, around and under the wire, back over the top of itself, and then under the wire again. Pull the knot in tight.

hitch knot Take the cord over the spring wire, around and under the wire, back over the top of itself, and then under the wire again. Bring it back over the top of the wire and through the second loop, pull the knot in tight.

locking/single knot Take a length of twine, make a loop with one end, take the same end back under and through the loop, and pull tight.

suppliers directory

suppliers directory

Suppliers have been listed by category, in alphabetical order. Please note some suppliers deal with trade only but will supply to retail outlets if requested, it is therefore recommended to confirm this on making contact with a supplier. The suppliers listed below include fabric for both upholstery and decorative purposes.

fabric and trimmings

Abbott & Boyd
1/22 Chelsea Harbour Design Centre
London, SW10 0XE, UK
tel +44 (0)20 7351 9985
fax +44 (0)20 7823 3127
www.abbottandboyd.co.uk
(distributed in the USA
by Brunschwig & Fils)

Altiplano
136 Sinclair Road, Garden
Studio, London, W14 ONL, UK
tel +44 (0)20 7603 0998
fax +44 (0)20 7602 2187
www.altiplano.co.uk
(selection of elegant and
contemporary braids and suede
trimmings and other suede and
leather products)

Alton Brooke
2/25 Chelsea Harbour Design Centre
London, SW10 0XE, UK
tel +44 (0)20 7376 7008
fax +44 (0)20 7376 7009
www.alton-brooke.co.uk

**Andrew Martin
International Ltd**
200 Walton Street
London, SW3 2JL, UK
tel +44 (0)20 7225 5100
fax +44 (0)20 7589 8502
email info@andrewmartin.co.uk

Unique Fabrics Ltd
6 Mt Eden Road, Eden Terrace
Auckland, New Zealand
tel +64 9 306 1580
(distributed in the USA
by Kravet)

Anna French
343 Kings Road
London, SW3 5ES, UK
tel +44 (0)20 7351 1126
fax +44 (0)20 7351 0421
www.annafrench.co.uk

Sanderson, D&D Building
979 Third Avenue
New York, NY 10022, USA
tel/fax +1 212 759 5408
www.ddbuilding.com

Interior Textiles Corporation
275 Swan Street
Richmond 3121, Melbourne,
Victoria, Australia
tel +61 39 428 1800
fax +61 39 428 0053

Crescendo, Annstarr Agencies
3–611 Alexander Street
Vancouver, BC BCA1E1
Canada
tel +1 604 254 3376
fax +1 604 254 3336

Baumann Fabrics
Worlds End Studios
134 Lots Road
London, SW10 0RJ, UK
tel +44 (0)20 7349 7022
fax +44 (0)20 7349 7024
www.creationbaumann.com

Création Baumann USA Inc
114 North Centre Avenue
Rockville Centre
New York, NY 11570, USA
tel +1 516 764 7431
fax +1 516 678 6848

Tessuti Uno
Création Baumann
Designer's Walk, DW Bldg 2
320 Davenport Road, Toronto
Ontario M5R 1K6, Canada
tel +1 416 922 0126
fax +1 416 922 0441

Création Baumann Pty. Ltd
214 Nicholson Street
PO Box 89, Fitzroy,
3065 Melbourne
Victoria, Australia
tel +61 39 419 6799
fax +61 39 417 4213

James Dunlop Textiles Ltd
PO Box 1636, Christchurch
New Zealand
tel +64 3366 8681
fax +64 3366 8790

Beaumont & Fletcher
showroom: 261 Fulham Road
London, SW3 6HY, UK
tel +44 (0)20 7352 5594
fax +44 (0)20 7352 3546
(istributed in the USA by
F. Schumacher & Co.)
www.beaumontandfletcher.com

office: 71 Warriner Gardens
The Old Imperial Laundry
London, SW11 4XW, UK
tel +44 (0)20 7498 2642
fax +44 (0)20 7498 2644

Bernard Thorpe & Co.
53 Chelsea Manor Street
London, SW3 5RZ, UK
tel +44 (0)20 7352 5745
fax +44 (0)20 7376 3640

Brunschwig & Fils Inc
C10 The Chambers
London, SW10 0XF, UK
tel +44 (0)20 7351 5797
fax +44 (0)20 7351 2280
www.brunschwig.com

D&D Building, Suite 1200
979 Third Avenue
New York, NY 10022, USA
tel +1 212 838 7878
fax +1 212 838 5611
www.ddbuilding.com

320 Davenport Road, Toronto,
Ontario, M5R 1K6, Canada
tel +1 416 968 0699
fax +1 416 968 6500

751 High Street, Armadale
Victoria 3143, Australia
tel +61 3 9509 6766
fax +61 3 9509 6866

Icon Textile Ltd, PO Box 9832
New Market /Level 2
155–165 The Strand
Parnell, Auckland, New Zealand
tel +64 9375 9850
fax +64 9375 9855

Colefax and Fowler
head office:
19–23 Grosvenor Hill
London, W1K 3QD, UK
tel +44 (0)20 7493 2231
fax +44 (0)20 7499 9910
for stockists:
+44 (0)20 8887 6400
(fabrics and trimmings;
distributor of Manuel Canovas
and Larsen)

Colefax and Fowler
110 Fulham Road
London, SW3 6HU, UK
tel +44 (0)20 7244 7427
fax +44 (0)20 7373 7916

see also:
www.chelsea-harbour.co.uk

for details of USA showrooms
(trade only):
Cowtan & Tout, 76 9th Avenue
New York, NY 10011, USA
tel +1 212 647 6900

for UK and worldwide
distributors:
tel +44 (0)20 8874 6468

Conran
Michelin House,
81 Fulham Road,
London,, SW3 6RD, UK
tel +44 (0)20 7589 7401
fax +44 (0)20 7823 7015
www.conran.com
(good selection of cotton
velvets and other neutral and
contemporary fabrics)

Bridgemarket,
407 East 59th Street,
New York, NY 10022, USA
tel +1 212 755 9079
fax +1 212 888 3008

Crowson
Crowson House, Bellbrook Park
Uckfield, East Sussex
TN22 1QZ, UK
tel +44 (0)1825 761044
fax +44 (0)1825 764283
(Distributor of Monkwell,
The Design Archives
and Hill & Knowles.)
www.crowsonfabrics.com

showroom:
227 Kings Road
London, SW3 5EJ, UK
tel +44 (0)20 7823 3294
fax +44 (0)20 7376 7767

Monkwell in the US:
tel +1 516 752 7600

Monkwell and Crowson in
Australia and New Zealand:
tel +61 295 189 911

Crowson (Australia) Pty Ltd
35–39 Mountain Street
Ultimo 2007, NSW, Australia
tel +61 29 211 7751
fax +61 29 211 7752

Crowson (New Zealandand) Ltd
PO Box 1303, Auckland,
New Zealand
toll-free in NZ: 0800 440 559
fax: 0800 440 576

Designers Guild
267 and 277 Kings Road
London, SW3 5EN, UK
tel +44 (0)20 7351 5775
fax +44 (0)20 7893 7620
www.designersguild.com
(distributed in the USA by
Osborne & Little)

head office:
3 Latimer Place
London, W10 6QT, UK
tel +44 (0)20 7893 7400
fax +44 (0)20 7893 7720

Radford Furnishing
Level 1, 146 Burwood Road
Hawthorn, Victoria 3122
Australia
tel +61 3 9818 7799
fax +61 3 9818 5531

Icon Textiles Ltd
Level 2, 155–165 The Strand,
Parnell, PO Box 9832
New Market
Auckland, New Zealand
tel +64 9302 1652
fax +64 9375 2855

Wellington Industries
Division Home Fabrics
60 Old Pretoria Road
Halfway House, Midrand
1685 Johannesburg, South Africa
tel +27 11 266 3700
fax +27 11 266 3900

Donghia
G23 Chelsea Harbour Design Centre
London, SW10 0XE, UK
tel +44 (0)20 7823 3456
fax +44 (0)20 7376 5758
www.donghia.com
(neutrals and classic
contemporary designs;
distributor of Anya Larkin)

Donghia Furniture/Textiles Ltd
485 Broadway
New York, NY 10013, USA
Tel : +1 212 925 2777
fax +1 212 925 4819

South Pacific Fabrics
(textiles, wallcovering, and trim)
195 Paddington Street
Paddington, NSW 2021, Australia
tel +61 2 9327 7222
fax +61 2 9327 3311

Atelier Textiles
(textiles, wallcovering, and trim)
55 Boston Road, Mt Eden,
Auckland, New Zealand
tel +64 9373 3866
toll-free in NZ: 0800 283 543
fax +64 9373 3566

Mavromac Pty Ltd (Textiles)
PO Box 76178
Wendywood 2144, South Africa
tel +27 11 444 1584
fax +27 11 444 1541

G.P. & J. Baker
2 Stinsford Road, Poole
Dorset, BH17 0SW, UK
tel +44 (0)1202 266 700
fax +44 (0)1202 266 701
www.gpjbaker.co.uk
(contemporary and printed
fabrics in neutrals and colours;
distributor of Parkertex;
distributed in USA by Lee Jofa)

showroom: G18–19,
Chelsea Harbour Design Centre
London, SW10 0XE, UK
tel +44 (0)20 7351 7760
fax +44 (0)20 7351 7752

Charles Radford Furnishings Ltd
8–18 Glass Street
Richmond 3121, Australia
tel +61 39 429 6122
fax +61 39 427 1587

Icon Textiles, PO Box 9832
Newmarket, Auckland,
New Zealand
tel +64 9302 1652
fax +64 9375 2855

Galbraith & Paul
116 Shurs Lane
Philadelphia, PA 19127, USA
tel +1 215 508 0800
fax +1 215 508 0866
(distributed in the UK by
Nina Campbell)

George Spencer Designs
29 Chapel Street
London, SW1X 7DD, UK
tel +44 (0)20 7235 1501
fax +44 (0)20 7235 1502
www.georgespencer.com
(make bespoke trimmings
enabling you to design your
own finish; good selection of
trimmings as well as innovative,
contemporary fabrics;
distributed in USA by
Claremont Furnishing Fabrics.)

Grand Illusions
41 Crown Road, St Margaret's
Twickenham, TW1 3EJ, UK
tel +44 (0)20 8607 9446
fax +44 (0)20 8744 2017
www.grandillusions.co.uk

Harlequin
Ladybird House, Beeches Road
Loughborough, Leicestershire
L11 2HA, UK
tel +44 (0)8708 300 356
fax +44 (0)8708 300 359
www.harlequin.uk.com
(colourful selection of
plain and patterned
contemporary fabrics)

Harlequin USA
5100 Highlands Parkway
Smyrna, Georgia 30082, USA
tel +1 678 303 9999
fax +1 678 303 8250

Beauport Wallcoverings
1400 Graham Bell, Boucherville
Quebec, J4B 6E5, Canada
tel +1 450 641 4477
fax +1 450 641 4585

Wilson Fabrics and Wallcoverings
Level 1, 10–14 Waterloo Street
Surrey Hills, New South Wales
2010, Australia
tel +61 2 597 7200
fax +61 2 597 7211

Malcolm Fabrics Ltd
PO Box 5460, Papanui
Christchurch, New Zealand
tel +64 3352 8668
fax +64 3352 6622

Bilchik Wallpapers Pty Ltd
33 Height Street, Doorn
Fontaine 2094, Johannesburg
2000, South Africa
tel +27 11 402 2800
fax +27 11 402 1151

Ian Mankin
109 Regents Park Road
London,, NW1 8UR, UK
tel +44 (0)20 7722 0997
fax +44 (0)20 7722 2159

retail:
271 Wandsworth Bridge Road
London, SW6 2TX, UK
tel +44 (0)20 7371 8825

Interiors With Flair
153 St Margaret's Road
Twickenham
Middlesex, TW1 1RG, UK
tel +44 (0)20 8255 1001
fax +44 (0)20 8255 1002
(good variety of
plain and patterned
contemporary fabrics)

**Jab International
Furnishings Ltd**
1/15–16
Chelsea Harbour Design Centre
London, SW10 0XE, UK
tel +44 (0)20 7349 9323
fax +44 (0)20 7349 9282
www.jab.de

Stroheim & Romann Inc
155 East 56th Street
New York, NY 10022, USA
tel +1 212 486 1500
fax +1 212 980 1782

JAB Anstoetz Inc
326 Davenport Road
M5R 1K6, Toronto, Canada
tel +1 416 927 9192
showroom: +1 416 920 3020
fax +1 416 927 7510

Seneca Textiles Ltd
317 High Street, 3181 Prahran
Victoria, Australia
tel +61 3 9529 2788
fax +61 3 9529 4388

Seneca Textiles (NZ) Ltd
14 Heather Street, Parnell
PO Box 37–702
Auckland, New Zealand
tel +64 9309 6411
fax +64 9309 8866

Chelsea Harbour Fabrics, Unit
17, Gallagher Place, Suttie Road,
Midrand, 1683 Midrand
South Africa
tel +27 11 315 9822
fax +27 11 315 9824

Jane Churchill
151 Sloane Street
London, SW1X 9BX, UK
tel +44 (0)20 7730 9847
fax +44 (0)20 7259 9189
(distributed in the UK and the
USA by Colefax and Fowler)

John Boyd Textiles
Higher Flax Mills, Castle Cary
Somerset, BA7 7DY, UK
tel +44 (0)1963 350451
fax +44 (0)1963 351078
www.johnboydtextiles.co.uk
(specialists in manufacturing
fabric made of horsehair; great
variety of colours; distributed in
the USA by F. Schumacher & Co.
Lee Jofa and Brunschwig & Fils)

showroom: Alton-Brooke, 2/25,
Chelsea Harbour Design Centre
London, SW10 0XE, UK
tel +44 (0)20 7376 7008
fax +44 (0)20 7376 7009
www.chelsea-harbour.co.uk

William Switzer & Associates
6–611 Alexander Street
Vancouver, BC V6A 1E1, Canada
tel +1 604 255 5911
fax +1 604 255 5931

Rata, 44 Ghuznee Street
Wellington, New Zealand
tel/fax +64 4801 9589

South Pacific Fabrics
195 Paddington Street
Paddington, NSW 2021, Australia
tel +61 2 9327 7222
fax +61 2 9327 3311

Knowles & Christou
116 Lots Road
London, SW10 0RJ, UK
tel +44 (0)20 7352 7000
fax +44 (0)20 7352 8877
www.knowles-christou.com
(beautiful hand-printed fabrics
and aesthetic furniture)

Kravet London
G/17
Chelsea Harbour Design Centre
London, SW10 0XE, UK
tel +44 (0)20 7795 0110
fax +44 (0)20 7349 0678
www.kravet.com
(good selection of neutral,
coloured, and textural
contemporary fabrics, faux
suede, and faux fur)

Kravet Inc Corporate
Headquarters:
225 Central Avenue South,
Bethpage, New York NY 11714,
USA
tel +1 516 293 2000
toll-free +1 800 645 9068
fax +1 516 293 2737
(distributor of Andrew Martin
International)

Tritex Fabrics Ltd
106–611 Alexander Street
Vancouver, BC V6A 1E1, Canada
tel +1 604 255 4242
fax +1 604 255 9255

Mokum Textiles, 98 Barcon
Avenue, Rushcutters Bay
Sydney, NSW 2000, Australia
tel +61 2 9380 6188
fax +61 2 9380 6476

Mokum Textiles Ltd
11 Cheshire Street
Parnell, Auckland, New Zealand
tel +64 9 379 3041
fax +64 9 377 5385

Larsen
1/12–13
Chelsea Harbour Design Centre
London, SW10 0XE, UK
tel +44 (0)20 7352 0047
fax +44 (0)20 7349 0700
Stockists: +44 (0)20 8877 6400
www.chelsea-harbour.co.uk
(distributed by Colefax
and Fowler)

Cowtan & Tout Larsen
20 Vandam Street
New York, NY 10013, USA
tel +1 212 627 7878

Lee Jofa
head office: 6 Stinsford Road
Poole, Dorset, BH17 0SW, UK
tel +44 (0)1202 266999
fax +44 (0)1202 266 766
www.leejofa.com
(decorative fabric, patterns,
and neutrals)

G/18–19
Chelsea Harbour Design Centre
London, SW10 0XE, UK
tel +44 (0)20 7351 7760
fax +44 (0)20 7351 7752
www.chelsea-harbour.co.uk

Lee Jofa Inc, 201 Central Avenue
South, Bethpage, New York
NY 11714, USA
tel +1 516 752 7600
fax +1 516 752 7623

The D&D Building
979 Third Avenue
New York, NY 10022, USA
tel +1 212 688 0444
fax +1 212 759 3658
www.ddbuilding.com
(distributor of G. P. & J. Baker,
John Boyd, Monkwell, and
Mulberry Home in the USA)

Lee Jofa Canada
Donovan & Associates Inc
Designers Walk, 320 Davenport
Road, Suite 200, Toronto
Ontario, MSR 2K9, Canada
tel +1 416 921 1262
fax +1 416 921 7875
(distributor of Mulberry Home)

Mokum Textiles (Lee Jofa)
98 Barcon Avenue
Rushcutters Bay
Sydney, NSW 2000, Australia
tel +61 2 9380 6188
fax +61 2 9380 6476

The Malabar Cotton Co. Ltd
31–33 The South Bank Business
Centre, Ponton Road
London, SW8 5BL, UK
tel +44 (0)20 7501 4200
fax +44 (0)20 7501 4210
UK stockists: +44 (0)20 7501 4200
www.malabar.co.uk
(colourful and large selection of
contemporary fabrics)

USA stockists:
+1 877 MALABAR

Australian stockists:
+61 2 9660 5588

WH Bilbrough & Co. Ltd
Designers Walk
362 Davenport Road, Toronto
Ontario, M5R 1K6, Canada
tel +1 416 960 1611
fax +1 416 960 5742

Halogen International
8 Kramer Road, Kramerville
Johannesburg, 2148, South Africa
tel +27 11 448 2060
fax +27 11 448 2065

Manuel Canovas
(large selection of velvet in
interesting colourways and other
contemporary fabrics; distributed
by Colefax and Fowler)

Mary Fox Linton
1/8–10
Chelsea Harbour Design Centre
London, SW10 0XE, UK
tel +44 (0)20 7501 7700
fax +44 (0)20 7720 0966
www.chelsea-harbour.co.uk
(strong collection of interesting
contemporary fabrics in neutrals
and patterns; distributor of Jim
Thompson, Glant, and Dedar)

Monkwell
showroom: 227 Kings Road
London, SW3 5EJ, UK
tel +44 (0)20 7823 3294
fax +44 (0)20 7376 7767
www.monkwell.com

Crowson House
Bellbrook Park, Uckfield
East Sussex, TN22 1QZ, UK
tel +44 (0)1825 761 044
fax +44 (0)1825 764 517

Mulberry Home
6 Stinsford Road
Poole, Dorset BH17 0SW, UK
tel +44 (0)1202 266 800
fax +44 (0)1202 266 801
www.mulberry.com
(distributed in Canada and the
USA by Lee Jofa)

Mulberry Home
showroom: 322 Kings Road
London, SW3 5UH, UK
tel +44 (0)20 7823 3455
fax +44 (0)20 7823 3329

Boyac Decorative Furnishings
537 High Street, Prahran East
Victoria, 3181, Australia
tel +61 39 533 7833
fax +61 39 533 8911
www.boyac.com.au

St Leger & Viney Pty Ltd
(Lee Jofa), PO Box 55508
Northlands 2116, Transvaal
South Africa
tel +27 11 444 6722
fax +27 11 444 6756
www.leejofa.com

Nina Campbell
trade showroom:
Bridge Studios
318–26 Wandsworth Bridge
Road, London, SW6 2TZ, UK
tel +44 (0)20 7471 4270
fax +44 (0)20 7471 4274
www.ninacampbell.com

retail: 9 Walton Street
London, SW3 2JD, UK
tel +44 (0)20 7225 1011
fax +44 (0)20 7225 0644
(distributed by Osborne &
Little; distributor of
Galbraith & Paul)

Osborne & Little
49 Temperley Road
London, SW12 8QE, UK
tel +44 (0)20 8675 2255
fax +44 (0)20 8673 8254
www.osborneandlittle.com
(distributor of Liberty
Furnishings and Nina Campbell)

304 Kings Road
London, SW3 5UH, UK
tel +44 (0)20 7352 1456
fax +44 (0)20 7351 7813

D&D Building, Suite 520
979 Third Avenue
New York, NY 10022, USA
tel +1 212 751 3333
fax +1 212 752 6027
www.ddbuilding.com
(distributor of Designers Guild
in the USA)

Primavera
160 Pears Avenue, Suite 110
Toronto, M5R 3P8, Canada
tel +1 416 921 3334
fax +1 416 921 3227

Mokum Textiles Pty Ltd
98 Barcom Avenue
Rushcutters Bay
NSW 2011, Australia
tel +61 2 9380 6188
fax +61 2 9380 6476
www.mokumtextiles.com

Mokum Textiles Ltd
11 Cheshire Street
Parnell, New Zealand
tel +64 9379 3041
fax +64 9777 5385

The Fabric Library
PO Box 912, Halfway House
1685 Johannesburg, South Africa
tel +27 11 265 9000
fax +27 11 315 1068

Parkertex
(distributed by G.P. & J. Baker)

Roger Oates Design
head office: The Long Barn
Eastnor, Ledbury
Herefordshire, HR8 1EL, UK
tel +44 (0)1531 631 611
www.rogeroates.com

shop: 1 Munro Terrace
Off Riley Street
London, SW10 0DL, UK
tel +44 (0)20 7351 2288

Romo
head office: Lowmoor Road
Kirkby in Ashfield
Nottinghamshire, NG17 7DE, UK
tel +44 (0)1623 756699
www.romofabrics.com

Arte Wallcoverings & Fabrics Inc
16758 West Park Circle Drive
Chagrin Falls, Ohio 44022, USA
tel +1(800) 338-ARTE

Marco Fabrics
155 Auburn Road, Hawthorn
Victoria 3122, Australia
tel +61 3 9882 7238

Seneca Textiles Ltd
14 Heather Street,
Parnell, PO Box 37-702,
Auckland, New Zealand
tel +64 9 3096 411

Sahco Hesslein
G24 Chelsea Harbour Design Centre
London, SW10 0XE, UK
tel +44 (0)20 7352 6168
fax +44 (0)20 7352 0767
www.sahco-hesslein.com
(strong collection of textures,
neutrals, wools, and cottons)

Bergamo Fabrics
PO Box 231, 256 Washington
Street, Mount Vernon, New York
NY 10553, USA
tel +1 914 665 0800
fax +1 914 665 7900
www.bergamofabrics.com

South Pacific Fabrics
195 Paddington Street
Paddington, NSW 2021
Australia
tel +61 2 9327 7222
fax +61 2 9327 7686
www.southpacificfabrics.com

Atelier Fabrics
55 Boston Road, Mount Eden
Auckland, New Zealand
tel +64 9 3733 866
fax +64 9 3733 566

Home Fabrics
60 Old Pretoria Road
PO Box 5207, Halfway House
Midrand 1685, South Africa
tel +27 11 266 3700
fax +27 11 266 3900
www.homefabrics.co.za

Sanderson
Sanderson House, Oxford Rd
Denham, UB9 4DX, UK
tel +44 (0)1895 830044
fax +44 (0)1895 830055
www.sanderson-online.co.uk

D&D Building, Suite 409
979 Third Avenue
New York, NY 10022, USA
tel +1 212 319 7220
fax +1 212 593 6184
www.ddbuilding.com

Telio & Cie
160 Pears Avenue, Suite 400
Toronto, Ontario, M5R 3P8
Canada
tel +1 514 842 9116
fax +1 514 842 3728

Australian Domestic Textile
Corporation Pty Ltd
95 Albert Street, Brunswick
Victoria 3056, Australia
Freephone: 1800 177 170
fax +61 3 9387 3338

Instyle Interior Products
37–41 Carbine Road
Mount Wellington, Auckland
PO Box 2312, New Zealand
tel +64 9574 3220
fax +64 9574 3221

The Fabric Library
PO Box 912, Halfway House
1685 Johannesburg, South Africa
tel +27 11 265 9000
fax +27 11 315 1068

Schumacher
F. Schumacher & Co.
D&D Building, Suite 832
979 Third Avenue
New York, NY 10022, USA
tel +1 212 415 3900
fax +1 212 415 3907
www.fschumacher.com
(distributed in the UK by Turnell
& Gigon; distributor of
Beaumont & Fletcher and John
Boyd in the USA)

Designer's Gallery
354 Davenport Road, Toronto
Ontario, M5R 1K6, Canada
tel +1 416 964 3714
fax +1 416 964 2015

Turnell & Gigon
Unit 2, Wellington Works
Wellington Road
London, SW19 8EQ, UK
tel +44 (0)20 8971 1711
fax +44 (0)20 8971 1716
(weaves, patterns, velvets, and
trimmings and braids;
UK distributor of
F. Schumacher & Co.)

G20 Chelsea Harbour Design Centre
London, SW10 0XE, UK
(contact numbers as above)

Victoria Bain
Unit 31, Pall Mall Deposit
124–128 Barlby Road
London, W10 6BL, UK
tel +44 (0)20 7207 8770
(embroidered fabric and braids)

V. V. Rouleaux
54 Sloane Square, Cliveden Place
London, SW1W 8AW, UK
tel +44 (0)20 7730 3125
fax +44 (0)20 7730 9985
www.vvrouleaux.com
(includes a large selection of
trimmings and braids)

Wemyss (Houlès)
Head Office: Baltic Works
Annfield Road
Dundee DD1 5JH, UK
tel +44 (0)1382 908 300
fax +44 (0)1382 908 308
(includes a strong collection of
braids, gimps, and trimmings)

1/20
Chelsea Harbour Design Centre
London, SW10 0XE, UK
tel +44 (0)20 7376 4430
fax +44 (0)20 7376 4465
www.chelsea-harbour.co.uk

Wendy Cushing Trimmings
G7
Chelsea Harbour Design Centre
London, SW10 0XE, UK
tel +44 (0)20 7351 5796
fax +44 (0)20 7351 4246
www.chelsea-harbour.co.uk
(wide selection of elegant and
opulent trimmings, also custom
made trimming service)

William Yeoward
270 Kings Road
London, SW3 5AW, UK
tel +44 (0)20 7349 7828
www.williamyeoward.com
(vibrant and interesting
contemporary fabrics focusing
on texture and colour)

Zimmer & Rohde
G13–15
Chelsea Harbour Design Centre
London, SW10 0XE, UK
tel +44 (0)20 7351 7115
fax +44 (0)20 7351 5661
www.zimmer-rohde.com
(selection of contemporary,
plain, and patterned fabrics)

D&D Building, Suite 1616
979 Third Avenue
New York, NY 10022, USA
tel +1 212 758 7925
fax +1 212 758 4372
www.ddbuilding.com

Tessuti Uno
320 Davenport Road, BL2
Toronto, Ontario, M5R 1K6
Canada
tel +1 416 922 0126
fax +1 416 922 0441

Locked Bag 1100
AUS-Edgecliff, New South Wales
2027, Australia
tel +61 02 9357 0555
fax +61 02 9380 6476

Zoffany
head office: Talbot House
17 Church Street
Rickmansworth
Herts, WD3 1DE, UK
tel +44 (0)8708 300 350

G9
Chelsea Harbour Design Centre
London, SW10 0XE, UK
tel +44 (0)20 7349 0043
fax +44 (0)20 7351 9677
www.zoffany.com
(chenilles and velvets)

Suite 1403, 979 Third Avenue
New York, NY 10022, USA
tel +1 212 593 9787
tel toll free 800 395 8760

Tessuti Uno
320 Davenport Road, BL2
Toronto, Ontario, M5R 1K6
Canada
tel +1 416 922 0126
fax +1 416 922 0441

Charles Radford
Level 1, Burwood Road
Hawthorn, Victoria 3122
Australia
tel +61 3 9818 7799
fax +61 3 9818 5531

Icon Textiles Ltd
Level 2, 155–165 The Str, Parnell
PO Box 9832, New Market
Auckland, New Zealand
tel +64 9302 1652
fax +64 9375 2855

leather, suede, and cowhide

Alma Home
Unit D, 12 - 14 Greatorex Street
London, E1 5NF, UK
tel +44 (0)20 7377 0762
fax +44 (0)20 7375 2598
www.almahome.co.uk
(suppliers of leather, suedes,
hides, and related products)

Andrew Muirhead & Son
Dalmarnock Leather Works
273–289 Dunn Street
Glasgow, G40 3EA, UK
tel +44 (0)141 554 3724
fax +44 (0)141 554 4741
www.muirhead.co.uk

**Coja Leatherline of
Canada Inc**
PO Box 185 Concord
Ontario, L4K 1Y6, Canada
tel +1 905 660 7600
fax +1 905 660 7592
www.coja.com

Elmo Leather
SE-512 81 Svenljunga, Sweden
tel +46 (0) 325 66 14 00
Fax +46 (0) 325 61 10 04
www.elmoleather.com

Elmo Leather, Inc.
505 Thornall Street, Suite 303
Edison, New Jersey 08837, USA
tel +1 732 549 5151
fax +1 732 549 7990

JMT Leather
1 Inca Business Park, Acton
Sudbury CO10 0BB, UK
tel +44 (0)1787 882552
fax +44 (0)1787 880 531

J T Batchelor Ltd
9-10 Culford Mews
London, N1 4DZ, UK
tel +44 (0)20 7254 8521
fax +44 (0)20 7254 0357

Leather Design
Riverside House
Easting Close, East Worthing
Trading Estate, Worthing
West Sussex BN14 8HQ, UK
tel +44 (0)1903 200 005
fax +44 (0)1903 532 565
(suppliers of cowhides and
related products)

Metropolitan Leather
Cottingham Way, Thrapston
Northants NN14 4PL, UK
tel +44 (0)1832 732216
fax +44 (0)1832 732 808
www.metropolitanleather.com
(suppliers of suede and leather)

**New South Wales Leather
Co. Pty Ltd**
707 Elizabeth Street
Waterloo, NSW 2017, Australia
tel +61 02 9319 2900
fax +61 02 9698 4747
www.nswleather.com

Walter Reginald
Unit 6, 100 The Highway
London, E1W 2BX, UK
tel: +44 (0)20 7481 2233
fax: +44 (0)20 7481 2255

upholstery suppliers

Benchmark
The 20th Century Theatre
291 Westbourne Grove
London, W11 2QA, UK
tel +(0)20 7229 4179
(suppliers of original antique-
style French studs)

B & M (Latex) Sales Ltd
169a High Street
Hampton Hill, Hampton
Middlesex, TW12 1NL, UK
tel +44 (0)20 8979 0457
(shop selling upholstery supplies,
foam cut to size)

The Easy Chair Co
30 Lyndurst Road, Worthing
Sussex, BN11 2DF, UK
tel +44 (0)1903 201081
(upholsterers and suppliers of
upholstery materials, large and
small orders, mail order
catalogue available)

Jill Saunders
46 White Hart Lane
London, SW13 0PZ, UK
tel +44 (0)20 8878 0400

(see also miscellaneous
addresses on page 171)

wood restoring suppliers

**British Antique Furniture
Restorers' Association
(BAFRA)**
The Old Rectory
Warmwell, Dorchester
Dorset DT2 8HQ, UK
tel +44 (0)1305 854822
www.bafra.org.uk

Jean Burhouse Furniture
The Old Sawmill, Dunkeld
Perth, PH8 0JR, UK
tel +44 (0)1350 727723
www.jeanburhouse.com
(suppliers of wood and craft
tools and materials including
wood restoration products)

Liberon Waxes
Mountfield Industrial Estate
Learoyd Road, New Romney
Kent, TN28 8XU, UK
tel +44 (0)1797 367555
www.liberonwaxes.co.uk
(suppliers of wood restoration
products including polishes,
waxes, cleaners and vanishes)

wood restorers

Twickenham Antiques
80 Colne Road, Twickenham
Middlesex, TW2 6QE, UK
tel +44 (0)20 8894 5555
www.twickenhamantiques.com
(full restoration service, along
with showroom offering
period furniture)

fire retardant companies

Essex Flameproofing
Unit 16, Arcany Road
South Ockendon
Essex, RM15 5TB, UK
tel +44 (0)1708 851885
www.essexflameproofing.co.uk
(offer flameproofing services
bringing fabric to fire retardant
standards)

Textiles FR
Unit 4b, Wharfdale Road
Euroway Trading Estate
Bradford, BD4 6SG, UK
tel +44 (0)1274 651230
www.textilesfr.co.uk
(offer flameproofing services
bringing fabric to fire retardant
standards)

upholstery cleaners

Carpet Magic
Oakdene Cottage, 74 Portmore
Park Road, Weybridge, Surrey
KT13 8HH, UK
tel +44 (0)1932 847770
(on site cleaning of upholstery)

KCP
Nightingale House
1–7 Fulham High Street
London, SW6 3JH, UK
tel +44 (0)20 8823 3532
(specialist interior cleaning
and Scotchgarding services,
upholstered furniture
cleaned on site)

**National Carpet Cleaners
Association**
62c London Road, Oadby
Leicester LE2 5DH, UK
tel +44 (0)116 271 9550
www.ncca.co.uk
(can supply names of local
companies that clean
upholstery)

auctions

ebay
www.ebay.com
(extensive online auction
including furniture and antiques)

Lawrences
Norfolk House, 80 High Street
Bletchingley, Surrey, RH1 4PA, UK
Tel; +44 (0)1883 743343
www.lawrencesbletchingley.co.uk
(large auction room with
monthly sales including a good
variety of antique furniture)

Lots Road Auctions
71 Lots Road
London, SW10 0RN, UK
tel +44 (0)20 7376 6800
www.lotsroad.com
(over 500 lots including
contemporary and antique
furniture auctioned each Sunday,
viewing previous four days)

Parkins
18 Malden Road, Cheam
Surrey, SM3 8QF, UK
tel +44 (0)20 8644 6633
www.parkinsauction.co.uk
(monthly auctions including
sales of antique furniture)

Phillips West
10 Salem Road
London, W2 4DL, UK
tel +44 (0)20 7229 9090
www.phillps-auctions.com
(regular auctions including
modern and antique furniture)

made to measure cushion pads

R D Putnam
Fryer's Works, Ground Floor
Abercrombie Avenue
High Wycombe, HP12 4AX, UK
tel +44 (0)1494 439616
(cushions sizes made to order
in feather pads and man
made materials)

antiques fairs and markets

Alfie's Antiques Market
13–25 Church Street
London, NW8 8DT, UK
tel +44 (0)20 7723 6066
www.egrays.com
(large covered market selling
antiques including furniture)

Bushwood Antiques
Stags End Equestrian Centre
Gaddesden Lane, Redbourn
Hemel Hempstead
Herts, HP2 6HN, UK
tel +44 (0)1582 794700
www.bushwood.co.uk
(extensive selection of
period furniture)

DMG Antique Fairs
PO Box 100, Newark
Notts NG24 1DJ, UK
tel +44 (0)1636 702326
www.dmgantiquefairs.com
(organizers of large, regular
antiques markets around the UK)

The Old Cinema
160 Chiswick High Road
London, W4 1PR, UK
tel +44 (0)20 8995 4166
www.theoldcinema.co.uk
(large showroom offering wide
selection of period furniture)

frame makers

J K Bone
404 Cremer Business Centre
Cremer Street, Shoreditch
London, E2 8HD, UK
tel +44 (0)20 7739 2470
(individual chairs made to
order by hand, offer a chair
matching service)

R G B Products
Gillmans Industrial Estate
Natts Lane, Billingshurst
West Sussex RH14 9EZ, UK
tel +44 (0)1403 783670
(chair and sofa frames made
to measure)

castors and furniture fittings

Brass Foundry Castings
Brasted Forge, Brasted
Kent TN16 1JL, UK
tel +44 (0)1959 563863
www.brasscastings.co.uk
(brass wheel castors matched or
copy cast)

Martin & Company (A.I.) Ltd
119 Camden Street
Birmingham, B1 3DJ, UK
Tel; +44 (0)121 233 2111
www.martin.co.uk
(selection of castors and fixtures)

miscellaneous useful addresses

**Association of Master
Upholsterers and Soft
Furnishers**
(incorporating the Chair Frame
Makers Association)
Frances Vaughan House
102 Commercial Street
Newport, Gwent NP9 1LU, UK
tel +44 (0)1633 215454
www.upholsterers.co.uk

AMUSF's USA representative:
Second Chance Upholstery
Patricia Gilkey & Donna Crawford
18904 Deer Hill Road, Middleton
California 95461, USA
tel +1 707 987 4477

**Association of Woodworking
and Furnishings Suppliers**
5733 Rickenbacker Road
Commerce, California 90040
USA
tel +1 323 838 9440
fax +1 323 838 9443
www.awfs.org
(can help source a wide range of
upholstery and wood-related
suppliers and services)

BADA (British Antique Dealers
Association)
20 Rutland Gate
London, SW7 1BD, UK
tel +44 (0)20 7589 4128
www.bada.org

British Standards Institute
389 Chiswick High Road
London, W4 4AL, UK
tel +44 (0)20 8996 9000
www.bsi-global.com

**Department of Trade
and Industry**
Ashdown House, 123 Victoria St.
London, SW1E 6RB, UK
tel +44 (0)20 7215 5000

LAPADA (London and Provincial
Antique Dealers Association)
535 King's Road
London, SW10 0SZ, UK
tel +44 (0)20 7823 3511
www.lapada.co.uk

**The National Council for
Vocational Qualifications**
222 Euston Road
London, NW1 2BZ, UK
tel +44 (0)20 7509 5555

**Association of Specialists
in Cleaning and Restoration**
8229 Cloverleaf Dr., Suite 460
Millersville, MD 21108, USA
tel +1 800 272 7012
fax +1 410 729 3603

Walnut
www.walnutuk.com
nicolefulton@walnutuk.com
tel +44 (0)1256 327400
(individual period chairs
sourced, restored, and
reupholstered in sumptuous
contemporary fabrics)

index

Page numbers in **bold** type refer to projects

acknowledgments

I would like to thank Catherine Emslie for her unstinting patience and good humour, Roger Dixon for his excellent photography and "cover all angles" approach, Stuart Weston for his craftsmanship and never ending patience, Carolyn Jenkins for bringing clarity to knots and stitches, Anna Sanderson for her guidance, Auberon Hedgecoe for his eye for detail and vision, Jo Weeks for her way with words, Colin Goody for his ingenuity, and Karen Hemingway for her initial expertise.

Grateful thanks to Damask for supplying their exquisite products: silk quilt, scatter cushions, white bed linen, and bedside table (as seen on pages 150 and 154). Damask can be found at: Broxholme House, New Kings Road, (by Harwood Road), London SW6 4AA; Tel: +44 (0)20 7731 3553, www.damask.co.uk, enquiries@damask.co.uk.

Thanks also to the two following books:
The Complete Upholsterer, Carole Thomerson (Frances Lincoln Ltd, London, 1989)
The Essential Guide to Upholstery, Dorothy Gates, (Merehurst Ltd, London, 2000)

Heartfelt thanks to each of the following fabric houses and suppliers for contributing some of the most sumptuous, fabulous, and innovative fabrics for use in the book. **Please note that some of the fabrics listed below are intended for decorative or light domestic use only, a barrier cloth or back coating may be required, and guidance should be obtained from the fabric supplier regarding suitability for upholstery purposes.**

Wing chair, front cover: Mary Fox Linton – *Manon*; trimming from VV Rouleaux
Spoonback chair from Walnut, p1: Mulberry – *Icedance*
Arts & Crafts side chair, p2 and p84: Anna French – *William 16*
Scatter cushion, p75: Andrew Martin – *Elvis (3127A)*
Bolster cushion, p76: Harlequin Jewel – *Adara J6709*
Box cushion, p77: Kravet – *CR Suede Chocolate*
Salon chairs, p80: Mary Fox Linton – *Fedra*; trimming from VV Rouleaux
Balloon-back dining chair, p86: J T Batchelor – Pony skin
Arts & Crafts easy chair, p90: George Spencer – *Makeba*; trimming from Turnell & Gigon
Sofa, p94: Harlequin (Jewel) – *Adara J6709*
Button-back chair, p98: Sacho Hesslein – *Elemento 1275-18*, and Kravet – *20911-16*
Leather club chair, p104: JMT Leather – *Barolo Expresso*, and Kravet – *CR Suede Chocolate*
French chairs, p110: Andrew Martin – *Woodstock Stone*
Wing chair, p114: Mary Fox Linton – *Manon*; trimming from VV Rouleaux
G plan chair, p122: Elmo – *Elmosoft VI 01061*
Box stool, p128 (also, fabric on p23): Metropolitan Leather – red pigskin suede, and Anna French – *William 6*, and
        Turnell & Gigon – *Veraseta Satin Latour 6037*; trimming from VV Rouleaux
Ottoman, p134: Walter Reginald – Cowhide
1970s "flower" stool, p138: Jab (Anstoetz) – *Monet Neu 1-6216-137* and SABA *1-6206-336*
Footstool with fitted cover, p142: Turnell & Gigon – *Velours Palace (gaufrage) 15523/0030*
Footstool with loose cover, p144: Donghia – *Eclipse 02*
Screen, p146: William Yeoward – *Hortense-Gooseberry* and Kravet – *14038 col 411*; trimming from VV Rouleaux
Shaped headboard, p150: Mulberry – *Icedance*
Panelled headboard, p154: Sacho Hesslein – *Dunes 1873-19* and Knowles & Chrisou – *Griffins Taffeta*

Picture credits
All pictures were photographed by Roger Dixon for Octopus Publishing Group Ltd with the exception of those appearing on pages 1 Nicole Fulton/Walnut; 6 Nicole Fulton/Walnut; 7 Interior Archive/Fritz von der Schulenburg; 8 centre left Narratives/Viv Yeo/British Trimmings; 8-9 Narratives/Jan Baldwin; 8-9 top Colefax and Fowler/Manuel Canovas; 9 bottom right Ray Main/Mainstream; 10 Nicole Fulton/Walnut; 12 Nicole Fulton/Walnut; 13 Nicole Fulton/Walnut; 22 Colefax and Fowler/Manuel Canovas; 24 bottom right Red Cover/Ken Hayden/Designer: Henri Becq; 25 top left Sahco Hesslein; 26 bottom right Nicole Fulton/Walnut; 27 top left Monkwell; 28 bottom right Sahco Hesslein; 29 top left Victoria Murray Public Relations; 30 bottom right Ray Main/Mainstream/Joseph; 31 top left From the Arc Collection by Harlequin Fabrics and Wallcoverings, telephone number 08708 300050; 32-33 Sahco Hesslein; 34 bottom right Colefax and Fowler; 35 top left Nicole Fulton/Walnut; 36 top left Sahco Hesslein; 36 top centre G. P. & J. Baker; 36 top right Lelièvre (UK) Ltd; 36 centre right Interior Archive/Photo: Fritz von der Schulenburg/Designer: De Padova; 36 bottom left Narratives/Tamsyn Hill/British Trimmings; 36-37 bottom Roger Oates Fabrics and Floors, www.rogeroates.com, telephone number 01531 531611; 37 top right Victoria Murray Public Relations; 37 centre right Interior Archive/Fritz von der Schulenburg/Designer: Chelsea textiles; 37 bottom right Nicole Fulton/Walnut; 156 top left Sahco Hesslein; 156 top centre Red Cover/Brian Harrison; 156 bottom left Interior Archive/Fritz von der Schulenburg/Designer: Chelsea textiles; 156-157 top Mulberry; 157 top right Victoria Murray Public Relations; 157 centre left Pierre Frey.